A HOUSE FULL OF WHISPERS

BY

SHARON WALLACE

Bloomington, IN Milton Keynes, UK

authorHOUSE®

AuthorHouse™
1663 Liberty Drive, Suite 200
Bloomington, IN 47403
www.authorhouse.com
Phone: 1-800-839-8640

AuthorHouse™ UK Ltd.
500 Avebury Boulevard
Central Milton Keynes, MK9 2BE
www.authorhouse.co.uk
Phone: 08001974150

This book is a work of non-fiction. Unless otherwise noted, the author and the publisher make no explicit guarantees as to the accuracy of the information contained in this book and in some cases, names of people and places have been altered to protect their privacy.

First published by AuthorHouse 6/21/2006

ISBN: 1-4259-4610-0 (sc)
ISBN: 1-4259-4611-9 (dj)

Printed in the United States of America
Bloomington, Indiana

This book is printed on acid-free paper.

Boarded Up

It's been many years I have stood empty alone
  I used to be somebody's home.

I hold many a dark secret some to hard to reveal,
  I had to watch and listen, as the family concealed.

He walked my corridors silent alone,
  forcing terror and tyranny in this three bed roomed home.

Children heard sobbing in the middle of the night
  I closed my doors, to hide their plight.

Humans have skeletons hidden so well
  the neighbours believe all was swell.

My windows darkened on the brightest of nights
  so no one will hear when he starts to fight.

He beat them all black and blue;
  I was brick and mortar what could I do.

So many secrets held behind my doors,
  so many little people whose lives he destroyed.

Now my shutters are up and my rooms lay bare,
  but the ghosts of the past will always be there.

❧ Chapter One ❧

"Go on then what you waiting for throw her in." my foster parent's jeered.

Confused and frightened by events taking place I looked to Paul my eldest brother for some answers, in his eyes I saw something I had never seen before, fear!

Both my brothers were dragging me naked towards the bushes, the ground scrapping my thighs as they dropped and dragged me towards their intended destination, swinging me to gain height I was thrown into the brambles and nettles, screaming hysterically I tried desperately to stand as brambles tore into my naked flesh, my feet cut from the stones as I grappled with my thorny landing my pleas ignored, they continued to laugh at my vulnerability.

Daddy-Beard lifted me onto the safety of the grass running to the security of my tent I was sure I was dreaming, unknown to me at that time both boys were being abused by them. Some thing I nearly stumbled across the night before my first day at school, unable to sleep I had almost walked into the unsavoury activities going on in the lounge, being young and having no call to fear them it was to go un-noticed.

I sat in my tent holding Molly Dolly for reassurance unsure what had just happened, or why.

My body burning as though a thousand hot needles were stabbing my delicate young skin, red wheels looking angry and sore covered the backs of my legs and buttocks.

Wrapping the sleeping bag around my nakedness I needed some sort of comfort, I could hear the family out side chatting as if every thing were ok, confusing me more, trying to find a patch of skin that did not hurt was proving difficult, as I slowly dressed.

Pushing my self far into the tent I did not want to go outside ever again, mother calling to come and put cream on made me tremble, dried blood adding to my fear I did not like these sorts of games.

"Sharon don't be a silly Billy this cream is magic, it will help the stinging to stop."

I went to the doorway of my tent making sure no one was either side of the entrance ready to pounce, quickly I ran towards mother, glancing to my brothers and yelling at the top of my voice

"I hate you two."

"Come on Sharon it was only a game, you have your clothes on inside out."

Mother was dabbing pink cream onto my skin

"Baby" Daddy-Beard teased.

"I don't love you, you were laughing at me." I pouted

"I am telling my teacher what you did."

"It was Paul and Mark darling, I did nothing."

Daddy-Beard protested his innocence

"YOU TOLD THEM TO DO IT."

Paul and Mark looked on in amazement I was not about to back down, "I promise it won't ever happen again darling, give daddy a cuddle."

All was forgotten as he gave me a hug and convinced me daddy was a hero, who rescued me from the jaws of my abusive brothers.

The holiday was filled with treats and fun, but also games, games that were to have distressing results on all three of us, thankfully I was not to be involved Paul and Mark did not have the same fortune.

We ate dinner and sang songs around the fire this was the first holiday we had as a family, until five months ago we had been raised in three different orphanages in as many years.

"Come on then time for bed." Mummy gently lead me to my tent tucking me into my sleeping bag, telling a story about a little girl who lives in the Forrest I listen intently to her, mummy's voice always soothing. Alone in my tent I lay and watch as her shadow disappears towards the camps fire. The silhouette of my parents lounging around talking in hushed tones makes my sleepy head, invite the sleepy dust that angels blow gently into my eyes.

The trees bending towards me as their shadows danced within the fires glow, I was sure the wind whispered my name laying with my head close to the entrance I snuggle up to Molly Dolly, the branches bend in the wind clutching outstretched, trying to lift me out of my bed invoking memories of the days events. An owl hooting in the darkness has me hiding in my sleeping bag, terror rocked my world and with Molly Dolly dangling precariously from my hand, I dashed to the safety of mummy and daddy.

"I want to stay in your tent."

Daddy-Beard led me back tucking me in tight, the sound of the zip closing was magnified by the silence of the dark, I watch his shadow disappear into the night and eventually I fall asleep as the day was dawning. My brothers happy when the tents were dismantled and we all climbed into the car for the journey home, our parents took delight in causing the boys distress I was starting to worry for them. Some times they were punished harshly, as with most children a parent's love is unconditional, silence can be bought with a few cuddles and a bag of sweets, and we accepted all.

The school holidays were drawing to a close Paul, would often listen to the banging and thumping beyond the forbidden doors of the garage, wondering what Daddy-Beard was doing, he was a mechanic and a very skilful person with his hands, making a beautiful dolls house and all the furniture for me, I believed he was a hero whom I loved very much. Appearing back in the garden he promised to take all three of us into the garage and show us a camper van he was restoring.

Lifting me onto his shoulders I always felt I was his princess, he made a special effort with me and apart from the camping trip I was never physically abused, it was not the same story for my brothers and they had started to resent me and my special treatment.

"Wow daddy it has a sink, look a cooker."

I had never seen anything like it captivating my imagination.

"One day when I am bigger I am going to buy one and drive all around the world, will you build me one daddy when I am a big girl."

"Anything for my princess, you have to let me travel with you"

"Don't forget to take us." Mark squealed

Each in turn he lifted us to see the inside allowing Paul and Mark to explore the garage, but warned them not to touch anything, I played in the dirt with a small dinky car the garage held no imagination for a little girl of five, Mark and Paul were six and seven years of age they excitedly scrutinised every thing.

"Time to go in I will clean up here and then we can go for a nice drive."

The boys were a little upset that the time spent was short, but I had seen enough and wanted to get back to my dolly.

We raced back to the house full of excited talk and patiently I sat on the back step waiting for Daddy-Beard to finish his work, I heard the doors slam

"Daddy that was quick."

He brushed past me his face angry and contorted I knew instantly my brothers were in trouble, he bellowed at all of us accusingly asking who had stood on the bumper.

We looked to each other with condemning stares

"Go and get my slipper I am going to teach you both a lesson you won't forget."

Mummy lifted me onto the kitchen work surface

"Trousers down you two stand in line Paul first."

The confrontation was scaring me as he raised his arm above his head, the slipper connected to the bare flesh of Paul's buttocks; he screamed out in agony Mark was terrified; he was made to watch knowing the fate that was awaiting him.

"Mummy, make him stop."

"Don't cry honey, he won't punish you we know you are too small to reach the bumper."

But that was not why I was crying Paul was my hero, my big brother and Mark, I was feeling their pain.

"Mark your next, I won't stop until one of you admits to standing on the bumper and leaving a bloody foot print on my new paint work" he was furious

Once again he lifted his arm above his head, Mark screeched in agony as the slipper connected to the intended target. This was too horrible for me to contemplate I wanted to get down and run into the garden.

"Stay her young lady watch and learn, see how the Lilly assed boys cry over nothing." Mummy was cold in her manner towards the boys suffering, almost enjoying the scene unfolding in front of her.

"Watch their cheeks glow they won't be sitting down for a while."

She was laughing demonically, mocking the terrified boys, taking delight in belittling them for the fear they were showing. It seemed to go on for hours each taking it in turn to be beaten, the sound of the slipper connecting with their bare flesh sickening what could I do? I was little no match for the grown ups.

"Did you do it?" he screamed once again

"No daddy"

Both protesting their innocence, each time made to bend and touch their toes, he was relentless I looked at Daddy-Beard and wanted him to drop dead.

Closing my eyes and placing my hands over my ears I tried to drown out the noises around me, every scream made me want to run I started humming gently, my eyes screwed tightly, but nothing worked I could still hear the sounds of my brother's cries and each individual connection of slipper to skin.

"It was me I did it." I confessed, knowing they would not hurt me physically, at worse I would be made to sit in my room both boys looked to me with anger.

"Don't lie Sharon how could you have."

"I don't know how I did it but I did."

I was made to go to my room and stay there, supper was bought on a tray my brothers blamed me for the terrible thrashing they had received, believing my admission of guilt.

That night Paul entered my room, pushing me down onto my bed he slapped me and said he would never forgive me, I should have said some thing sooner before they were hit.

He took my precious Molly Dolly and snapped off her head, he had never shown fury and hatred like this before I did not tell our parents, afraid what they would do to him. Daddy mended Molly's head but I was never going to leave her alone again.

The school we attended noticed Mark had become withdrawn Paul, was getting more aggressive towards his peers, and I very quiet. After yet another violent tantrum from Paul, towards his form teacher it was decided to send him to a doctor where he disclosed the abuse both he and his brother were suffering.

They notified the authorities and we were placed back into local authority care, no explanation was given why we no longer had a home or either parent. Mummy explained she had a bad back and needed to rest, when her back was better she would come and take us home.

We were allowed two toys to take with us; this was fine by me I believed we were to return home soon.

I chose my stuffed monkey and my treasured Molly Dolly, Paul and Mark refused to take anything, only their clothes.

I took a long time to settle and was upset when leaving school, watching the children running to their parents being swept into their arms just like my mummy used to.

Each day was filled with hope and a wish that today was the day mummy and daddy would be taking me home, each night I would kneel beside my bed and pray for them to come wondering what I had done wrong.

What was so wrong that no one could love me? Mark and Paul were happy to be safe, Paul decided he never wanted a family again and Mark was of the same opinion me, I yearned to have a family it was my birthday and Christmas wishes.

We settled once more to life in the orphanage and over the following months we became inseparable, the divide once felt between us at the Beards forgotten, Mark and I looked to Paul for guidance. All of us were called to the office and informed that the boys were being moved, it was arranged for the following morning. We had no say in the matter and I thought my heart would break when the time came to say goodbye. We all cried and hung onto each other as they dragged us apart, I started to get hysterical refusing to let go of them, I was to be on my own once again, when the car arrived to take me to a new home I did not participate in the journey, choosing to close my eyes and mind to the days events.

Looking to all the adults around me I loathed each one and blamed all for my loneliness, again I settled into the routine of yet another home feeling increasingly unhappy and missing my brothers terribly, withdrawing from playing and interacting with the other children and then ceased eating, becoming quite weak.

Christmas and the hustle and bustles of the preparations could not hold my attention, the decision was made to move me to the boys until a place could be found for all three, we had been apart for nearly seven months a long time for a child of seven years of age.

We hugged and danced my brothers showed me around the grounds it was exciting, I kept touching them to make sure it was not a dream, a very large wood stretched around the outside boundary of the orphanage, and we fantasized about running away and making a den.

"We could live here for ever no one would be able to split us up ever again." Paul chuckled.

The blue bells carpeted the woods and the spiders webs resembled jewels in the morning's mist, I could not contain my pleasure at last my brother's were once more with me, I was given a room at the top of the house, being the only girl I had a room to myself and climbing the winding staircase I could feel the hairs on my neck stand up, all around seemed dark and eerie I have a vivid imagination it was working over time.

A wooden bed stood alone in the corner, the floorboards bare and echoing each footstep one cupboard for my clothes, a little window with small panes of glass stood cacophonously on the wall as if it were a second thought to the building, but the view was pleasant, I could see above the trees and beyond the hill. Sitting on the bed dangling my feet Molly Dolly, was placed lovingly on my pillow deciding to return down stairs to find Paul.

"I don't like the room."

"Don't worry Sharon I will sneak up tonight and stay with you for a while."

True to his word Paul and Mark regularly checked that I was ok.

"I need to go for a pee."

I said crossing my legs tightly trying to balance on one foot.

"You are not allowed down stairs after dark." Paul informed

"What am I going to do?"

"Be quiet some one is coming."

Paul dashed under the bed and I jump into it

"You awake Sharon." it was Mark

"Where's Paul."

"I am here I thought you were the masters, Sharon needs to pee do you think we can make it down the stairs without being seen?"

"Oh hell Sharon why didn't you go before you came to bed? You know no one is allowed to walk around the house at night."

"I did not want to go then." I started to sob

"Its ok, take of your dressing gown and pee on it I will hang it out of the window and dry it for you."

I started to pee but it was going every where the patter of urine hitting the floor was loud, amplified by the lack of furniture in the room.

"Shush… slow it down." Mark whispered.

"Bloody hell Sharon it sounds like rain."

We all started to giggle Mark kept an eye on the door while I finished, and Paul ran around looking for some thing to mop the mess up.

We hung the gown out of the window, leaning on the windows ledge looking out at the views the night has a way of hiding all the lands indiscretions, silence fell as we captured the stillness and beauty before us. The moon shone bright cascading its light over the grounds, the stars shone like jewels twinkling in the cold March sky.

"Look at the stars I wonder if we could touch them if we climbed on the roof?"

Our train of thought was disturbed by the dressing gown floating towards the ground below.

"Bloody hell, Jesus Christ, Shit! Shit!"

"Paul! THAT'S NAUGHTY WORDS you will never go to heaven."

"I AM THE ELDEST, so I am allowed, what we going to do now?"

"We will get it in the morning, what's that over there?" Mark added excitedly.

A small door half way up the wall in the corner of the room stood ominously before us, it was almost touching the ceiling.

"That's a silly place to put a door, Paul how are we supposed to get in it?"

"I don't know."

We started to look around the room the moon lit the four corners like a trailing dust storm.

"I have never noticed the door before." Mark sounded puzzled.

"It has always been there but I don't like it." I informed the baffled boy's.

"I think the goblin lives in there with the pixies and fairies" I added.

"There's no such thing as fairies" Mark snapped

"There is too the tooth fairy left sixpence under my pillow" I argued.

"Help me with the bed Mark, if you stand on my shoulders I can lift you up, and then you can open the door and have a look in."

They enthusiastically moved the bed excitement taking over the worry of being heard, Mark was too heavy for Paul to hold.

"Ok Sharon, on the bed and let Mark stand on your back."

I dutifully did as ordered but was worried about whom, or what lived in such a small space. Mark stood on my back my hands and legs collapsed, we both laughed as we tumbled off the bed onto the floor.

"You're too heavy for me lets just leave it, there may be a monster kept up there, that's why the doors so small they made it small and higher up to stop him getting out."

"NO THEY DID'NT stop saying that it's just a cupboard I bet, you're just a silly girl."

Paul was a little unsure it seemed exciting at first but having a monster in there did not come into his thoughts.

He was nine years of age and a big boy too old to be scared by monsters; well that's what he believed. What he was thinking and so was Mark, treasure, buried in the attic for years waiting to be found by them, they would be rich beyond their wildest dreams.

"Put your hands together Sharon and let Mark stand on them."

"You want me to give him a bunk up?"

"Yes, do you think you will be able to do that."?

"I can try, come on Mark."

Mark managed to grasp the edge of the door and gingerly pulled, Whoosh, the door flew open easier than any expected Mark screamed sure some one from inside had opened it; we were surprised how easy it had been. No one spoke we looked at the dark hole that was once a door, I made sure that both brothers were in front of me

"What now."

"Now we go and find the treasure, come on I will get in first then I will pull Mark up, we can both pull you."

The boys seemed to scramble in with ease fuelled by the excitement of hidden treasures.

"Come on Sharon give us your hands stretch, that's right walk up the wall you can do it."

Paul and Mark pulled me into the doorway.

"Wow, its dark what if some one else is in here ready to eat us"

"LETS GO." Mark turned to leave

"It's to dark to see anything in here we will get in trouble"

"Yellow belly" Paul teased.

He was just as anxious but was not about to show it.

"We will leave the door open so we can jump out if any one is here." he tried to reassure.

I started to see shadows as my eyes adjusted to the dark

"What's that?" I panicked

"There's some one stood there, see! See"!

Marks voice started to rise from a whisper to a high pitch, the smell from the attic was dusty and old, we were holding onto each other willing each to walk in front the creaking floorboards added to my imagination of ghosts and goblins living here. We approached the shadow who was watching, Paul ordered me to speak.

"Hello, I am Sharon this is Mark and Paul."

"BLOODY HELL Sharon I don't think he wants our names."

I started to cry my body shaking my teeth chattering, Paul started to run his hands along the walls.

"What are you doing?" Mark whispered anxiously.

"Looking for a light switch I think that's just a dummy because it has not said anything."

"Or he could be waiting for us to split up so he can guzzle us separately."

I frantically searched for a light switch rubbing over the wall with open palms afraid I may touch some thing alive.

"Please god, help us find a light switch." I repeated over and over.

"Sharon, stop making me laugh."

I found nothing funny going on here and the thought that Paul was laughing totally perplexed me.

"Just keep talking to me so I can hear your voices."

I was beginning to panic, the darkness as black as ebony the unfamiliar ground afoot was getting too much to cope with.

"What's this... Ah

Hearing Marks cries I headed for the doorway not realizing how far away it had become, suddenly a blast of light lit the attic I stopped and looked around and could never remember being this afraid, clasping my hand over my eyes the sudden light blinding.

"Mark, Paul, where are you? I want to get out of here." I was crying uncontrollably the monster had eaten them my eyes adjusting to the brightly lit room I heard moaning, Mark, and Paul, were rolling on the floor and they sounded as though they were in pain.

I was rooted to the spot with fear and believed they had been attacked; hovering above them was the eyes of a ten foot monster his furry arms raised above his head ready to strike the boys.

"I will get help hold on." petrified I started towards the doorway loosing control of my bladder my pyjamas stuck to my legs.

"Wait Sharon Hang on, we are ok."

"We are laughing at you and your monster, look."

I stopped, but was afraid to turn I knew what I had seen and it was not of this world, gingerly I turned and came face to face with the alien inside, it was a bear, an old stuffed bear with a straw hat, for the first time I looked around relieved the monster was no more, and a stuffed bear stood in its place. The attic was crammed full of boxes and cases it was a magical place, pictures stacked along the walls a few old desks and chairs, it looked abandoned no one had been here for a long time.

There were various stuffed animals, with the bear stood a tiger and lion and some little rabbits, I found a tiny mouse that was raggedy in appearance his fur missing and also a leg, and straw hanging out of its back where the material had thinned through time.

"Is this Africa?" I asked walking around the array of stuffed animals confused by their existence.

"Don't be stupid Sharon, Africa." Paul mocked my naivety.

"Stop laughing at me I am not listening to you."

I thought back to Molly my best friend when I was four, her compelling stories took me to her native Africa where the elephants gazelles lions and rhino's all roamed free, animal's I had never seen. Molly would go into great detail about the elder's who ate monkeys and rats and in Africa it was a delicacy and eaten with relish, I never tired of Molly's stories.

I claimed the mouse as my own it had pride of place on my pillow next to my beloved Molly Dolly.

"How did you find the light?"

"I thought you were not talking to me." Paul teased.

"I did." Mark jumped in feeling gallant

"The monster that touched my face it was a light switch when I pushed it off my face I turned it on, look."

Mark pulled the string turning the lights on and off. Both started laughing again at the sight of me running to get help, I was still apprehensive and a little angry they were laughing at my uneasiness.

I picked up the stuffed rabbits and hurled them at my brothers, this only added to their amusement.

"We will get into trouble for being here if you two don't shut up."

"Then we won't tell any one this will be our secret Mark, do you agree?"

"Yes, it's our den look a train." he was distracted by his treasures.

"Swear you won't tell any one Sharon, if you do I will pull your dolls head off again."

"I won't, you leave Molly Dolly alone." I scolded with both hands firmly on my hips.

"Look at all these things lets open some boxes."

Paul was getting excited about being right

"See I told you there would be treasure look, try this on!"

Mark handed me a dress, I got out of my wet night clothes and dressed in the flowing gown.

We stayed for a few hours our imaginations took us to far away lands it became our secret hiding place, a little world invaded by no one and nothing.

Many hours were spent in the attic it allowed us to escape the rejection of our families, and the sadness of what had been lost. Within a few months a place was found in another home we were sad to leave our private little world, but happy to be together.

⊰ Chapter Two ⊱

THE NEW ORPHANAGE WAS IN WALES A LOVELY PART OF the country, we were nervous about meeting other people especially the boys, Mr and Mrs Cheese ran the orphanage and we were advised to call them Aunty Kay and Uncle Jim. Mark asked if there was an attic and we were informed yes but to dangerous for children,

"You will have to play either in the play room or the garden."

It was a very big garden and had a large menagerie of chickens, geese and cockerels, an apple and pear orchard and the longest grass I had ever seen.

I loved the smell of grass on hot summer days especially when it had just been cut, I found a toy car with red padded seats that was worked by battery and when fully charged went like the wind, many hours were spent driving around my imaginary world in which I escaped.

We settled quickly due to the care and attention that was given us, since leaving our foster parent's Paul, had become protective towards Mark and I, and very bossy; some times he would hit me mimicking the violence he suffered.

I was the victim of his behaviour and on our way to school some times hitting me if I refused to do as he ordered.

Arriving at school one of the teachers noticed I was upset.

"What's wrong Sharon? Oh dear come here."

She was gentle and caring lifting me into her arms and cuddling me making me feel safe, I never revealed why I was crying the memory of the terrible thrashing both my brothers suffered at the hands of our foster dad, was still fresh in my mind. Paul was reacting to the violent situation we had lived, thinking violence was the way to get what was needed.

He held enormous anger feeling he was to blame for not protecting us, misguided as this was, no one asked us what we wanted we were moved on the assessment of Paul, Mark was quiet and slightly withdrawn, analyzing each situation before making a decision. He had lost the ability to act on impulse, I was afraid if voices were raised or if there was any suggestion of a confrontation. The attention from my teacher made me feel a little special, some mornings I would pretend to be upset just to have a cuddle, just wanting to be loved.

So each of us were learning at a young age to manipulate, many things had happened to us things no child should have to endure, pictures no child should be able to see, emotion's no child should be made to feel.

Respite from all our problems was the seaside a place I loved my special place, go-carts and buggy rides the excitement of sleeping in a caravan. Wanting my own family was still my hearts desire, I watched the families and craved to be some ones daughter.

Before the Beard's fostered us we had no concept of family life and no desire to belong, we felt strong with each other and bonded well, since being taken back into care a real family became my Christmas, and Birthday wishes.

Like most children we hung onto the love and attention shown, abuse is masked and forgotten when an act of kindness is shown

"When I am married I am going to live by the sea." I adamantly informed my aunt.

All good things must come to an end it was time to return home and get things ready for another school term.

The night before school term started I began having stomach pains but no one believed me, I had lied and feigned illness to stay at home a few times last term.

"Come on young lady you have to go to school."

"But I really do feel poorly."

It was no good like the boy who cried wolf I was going to learn a hard lesson, at school the pain kept coming and going so even the teachers were unsure whether I was indeed ill.

Returning home I went straight to my room I had soiled my underwear, although we had never been punished harshly and never had any reason to fear Aunty Kay or Uncle Jim, I worried about doing such a filthy thing, hiding my underwear seemed a good choice and I would ask Paul what to do later, he would help. I fell asleep exhausted from my day the pain getting duller. Some time later I heard someone calling I felt as though I was in a long tunnel, and try as I might I had no energy to rise from my slumber.

The next thing I remembered was waking in the hospital with two women sat by my bed. I asked who they were and the smallest lady started to stroke my hair, I liked this type of attention and soaked it up as a sponge.

"Hello you I am a helper I visit poorly little boys and girls, how are you feeling."

I liked her straight away but was too weak to answer drifting back into a hazy sleep, listening to the sounds of the woman's voices.

"You would think with her mother living just down the road she would have visited."

"I would if it were my child."

My appendix had been removed and for a while I was very ill, it had been touch and go whether I would pull through, emergency surgery had been preformed with out me waking up since collapsing at home, I was missing my brothers but also thriving on the attention I was receiving from the nursing staff.

It felt nice to be cuddled and wanted I was not too keen to give all this attention up; it had been three weeks since last seeing them.

Paul and Mark was allowed the day off school to be there when I arrived home, on returning I asked Paul about mother, and what I overheard. He explained we were orphans and that we had no parents, both had been killed when we were very small instinct told me he was not telling the truth, he seemed hurt whenever I raised the subject.

Giving different stories each time when asked there were also memories; I could remember little things.

A man in uniform that used to visit and take me to see some other children, his smell a nice clean smell this adult was important but who was he I had no idea, I was able to recall most things about him but not his face and no matter how hard I tried I could never see it. There was also another time when about four years old; I remembered standing by a door watching a large lady arguing with a man, the man was familiar to me he wore a hat and a long coat and was asking to visit, the lady was crossly telling him no, after the door was closed I ran to the window and watched as he walked out of the gates, it was then I also noticed a lady accompanied him.

Still wanting to be someone's daughter school time was the worst, watching the children being picked up from school getting into their parents' cars, while I and the rest of the children walked alone with no one's hand to hold, no busy gossip on the day's events.

Christmas was soon upon us and we were informed we may choose one new present, and were asked to write a list one present from our list would be purchased. I wrote a Tressy doll, this doll had magical hair that would grow and I had seen it advertised on the television. My second choice a white fluffy mechanical dog, when wound with a key did cute somersaults and sat and barked, these were the only things I wanted, Paul looked out of the window

"It's snowing look every one."

We all ran to the window and watched as large snowflakes started to fall, another week and Christmas would be here.

"I suppose we should go and get the tree before we are snowed in, every one get you hats and coats, don't forget your mittens and boots."

Aunty Kay was bellowing the orders the older children rushed with excitement, we were ushered into the mini-bus I had just turned eight, and was classed as an older child; this was my first year to help choose the tree.

A joint decision would be made which tree to chop that would take pride of place in the playroom, the conversation and atmosphere on the bus was electrifying, I was captivated by the beauty of the landscape that unfolded before me, although darkness came early in winter the heavy snowfall bought an eerie brightness to the countryside, a perfect picture postcard. Deep snow carpeted the ground blown into drifts by the biting easterly winds, as the doors to the mini bus were opened the cold snap of the outside air burned into our faces. This had to be my favourite time of year.

I ran with the others looking for the best tree each one ahead looked better than the last.

"This ones the best" Sally shouted,

"No this one" Mark said adamantly,

THIS ONE, WHICH ONE, was all that could be heard from the children as we ran from tree to tree, after debating for a while and Aunty Kay refereeing with decorum, we all decided what we chose, was the biggest and best. It was getting bitterly cold my ears were tingling and the flakes were freezing to my woollen gloves, snow crunched beneath my feet as we struggled with the tree, at last it was secured to the roof of the mini bus ready to take home. I was still very small and hung onto the tree so tightly I was lifted with it and rescued from my fate by the dashing woodsman.

"Good job the man helped to load it."

Uncle Jim sighed, he was exhausted from trying to get every one to lift in unison, we sang carols on the way home there was a lot of sniffles and sneezing from the cold nights air, tired of wiping the wet window that was obstructing my view, I sat and listened to the others all getting into the festive mood, after helping to get the tree inside we were all given a mug of soup.

The tree filled the whole corner from floor to ceiling and was dressed and glittered all over, the fairy stood at the top of the tree looking down on the bright lights that adorned all branches. We all helped to make the decorations for the ceiling from sticky paper, this was a yearly ritual and although it was always the same, we never bored of it.

Every one went to bed tired that night the hour was some thing we were not used to, but it was a nice tired feeling, the week ahead was filled with the hustle and bustle of Christmas concerts, held at the school, and preparations for the coming church service that all attended on Christmas day.

It was soon Christmas Eve the younger children were getting

very excited, they had checked many times to make sure Santa's biscuit and glass of milk had been left for him in the kitchen. We were allowed to stay up later this night, it was a special holiday and the local church would be having a service at midnight for who ever wanted to attend. I was now given the choice if I would like to go, declining I knew if you see Santa bringing the presents he would take all the presents back, so I was going to make sure I was fast asleep.

"Quickly Sharon go to sleep Santa's on his way if you peek at him he won't leave your presents."

This had been said in all the orphanages I had lived nearly every year when excitement was stopping me from sleeping.

Even Daddy Beard had said it so it must be true; the children were tucked up in bed the gardener had been asked to clear the snow away from around the house, when it thawed it could flood the down stairs and six feet of snow and over was not unusual.

I could not sleep with the thrill of the coming day, looking out of my bedroom window the snow had stopped falling for a while, the orchard glistened like a thousand diamonds in the moon light, the trees covered in snow their branches bowing with the weight of the last storm, the lights from the rooms down stairs shadowed onto the garden below giving out a warm glow of yellow. Watching the gardener clearing a path for the people going to midnight mass, I thought about the foster parents and what they would be doing right now. Looking towards the stars there was an aching in my heart, remembering what Daddy Beard had said the last time I saw him.

"When ever you are feeling sad or afraid darling, look to the stars and I will also be looking, you will always be here with me"

He placed the palm of his hand over his heart, I brushed the single teardrop from my cheek this was a magical time, every thing seemed clean and snow bought freshness and brightness to the once dull and dreary surroundings that winter months bring.

Climbing back into my warm snug bed the blankets felt heavy and safe, I fell asleep that chilly December night my dreams filled with magical images only a child could dream. Christmas morning the children woke early a small gift of chocolate, and a piece of fruit was always left on the beds from Santa Claus, squealing from the younger children ran through the house. We all waited on the landing; Aunty Kay would not allow any one down stairs alone, we could hear the cook buzzing around in the kitchen and the clatter of the dishes as the tables were being laid.

Some of the children sat with their legs dangling precariously through the banisters singing carols, others were excitedly talking about the waiting array of gifts they were hoping for, I looked over to my brothers they were deep in conversation, I thought about Christmas together as a family with the Beard's, this was so different, my heart started to feel heavy again wishing I were there with them.

"Come on then, you may come down." the cook shouted up to the eager faces of the children, we had to eat breakfast first before opening our gifts, no one wanted to eat.

The gifts were set out in large white sacks with the names of each child sown into them, the dinning room and the playroom were divided by two large white doors, when opened both rooms became one big room.

These doors were only opened on birthdays and Christmas, when the children raced into the dinning room they were able to see the many sacks of toys in the playroom, waiting for young hands to eagerly open the brightly wrapped gifts. The younger children sat side ways on their chairs scanning the room for a sign where their presents were, too excited to think of food all things were done in an organized way; again this was a reminder of Christmas as a family with the Beard's, I was able to compare my life now to another.

"You may go and open your presents." there was a surge of small bodies rushing to the playroom, the anticipation of what Santa had bought over whelming for us all.

Reaching into my sack hoping for Tressy the toys had no original packaging, but brightly coloured Christmas paper, many of the gifts were donated by the families who lived in the surrounding areas, but the children were not aware of this.

"A Cindy doll wow, look Mark I have a Cindy doll."

He did not respond to me, he was busy enthusiastically diving into his own toys, nearing the bottom of my sack there was a nice new fluffy dog, I wound his key and watched as he playfully barked and somersaulted.

"Sharon what about your others presents?"

aunty was trying to get all the children to finish opening their presents; time was moving on all had to be dressed and ready for church in a few hours, over whelmed with my little dog I had forgotten the rest of my gifts.

Digging deeper I felt a hard pair of legs holding my breath daring for it to be the doll I had asked for, shaking with expectation I opened the gift with batted breath and ripping at the wrapping as though I were possessed, praying hard for what I had wanted all year.

Yes it was Tressy I looked and admired the doll my eyes wide with excitement, on closer inspection I was horrified to discover one arm missing, I searched the sack over and over scanning the floor meticulously. Examining the doll further Tressy's blonde hair was shorter than should be, I inspected the doll thoroughly; there was a hole at the top of the head where her hair should be.

Trying all I could to dig into her head to find her missing hair but to no avail, I took it to aunty

"My Tressy has an arm missing, I can't find it."

"It will be fine Sharon, just think of her as a special Tressy."

That snippet of advice would have been fine for a baby, but I had just turned eight years of age I started to get anxious,

"Her hair won't grow when I turn the knob on her back." raising my voice with antagonism, demonstrating to her how the hair was suppose to be pulled from the top of the head as the knob on Tressy's tummy was turned, welling up with tears my vision becoming blurred I had never felt this angry.

"Some one has cut Tressy's hair, SHE IS BALD" the horror of the situation dawning on me.

"Why has Santa given me a broken Tressy?"

I threw her across the room in frustration, all year apart from a few misunderstanding I had been trying hard to be good, recently wondering if there really was a Santa, but after being told that if you don't believe he won't leave you any thing I had changed my mind.

"Go and pick her up, I will have a word with Santa I am sure we will be able to sort it out."

I refused obstinately to obey, Mark ran over picked up the doll and handed her to me, again I threw the doll and slumped into the chair crossing my arms rebelliously, anger seared through my body I wanted to scream.

"Stupid Santa, stupid Tressy, stupid everything."

Tressy vanished into thin air never to be seen or spoken of again, we were warm and well fed but it wasn't the same as being part of a family.

The New Year bought new adventures I was old enough to join the brownies and admired my reflection in the mirror, proud of the smart uniform the beret placed on my head with pride; the activities given to gain brownie points bought out my competitive streak. Brown owl was explaining a swimming gala to raise money for charity; all those interested were to write their names and would be informed when practice takes place.

I excitedly scribbled my name in my best handwriting eagerly telling Aunty Kay about my new activity

"Can you swim Sharon?"

"Of course I can, like a brick my aunty Sally once told me." Aunty Kay laughed

"A brick! Some times Sharon you are amusing."

All practice sessions were held at brown owls home in her private pool, it was decided that I were to be in the relay team, being one of the weaker swimmers and youngest.

Swimming was more difficult than I had imagined tiring very easily, as long as I had one leg on the bottom of the pool bouncing along all would be fine.

The day of the gala arrived and all the children were excited, especially me, this was the first time I had attended any function out side of the various orphanages we had lived.

"Make sure you have your costume and towel, oh and don't forget your bathing cap."

Aunty Kay called as I danced around the playroom.

The children piled into the mini bus arriving in time to see the other teams queuing out side.

"See you inside Sharon good luck."

We were all checked in and names and address given on entry.

"What's your name then miss?" the man at the door inquired.

"I am Sharon Arscott." I beamed with pride

"And your address?"

"Umm I don't know." I looked towards brown owl as the man beckoned her over,

"This little girl seems to have forgotten her address."

"Sharon Arscott and she lives at, now let me see."

Fiddling in her bag pulling out a piece of paper,

"Yes here it is I thought I had it some where."

Opening the folded paper, brown owl proceeded.

"Home for Waifs and Strays, St Caddick's house, Carleon."

The man looked questionably at brown Owl and then sympathetically to me, I felt a little shy of his reaction, but was intrigued by home for waifs and strays, what on earth could that mean.

"Ok Sharon you may go inside"

I walked into the changing rooms clutching my bag, the smell of chlorine and the echoing sound of the children prattling and laughing excitedly whilst changing into their swimming costumes, added to the excitement.

I was going to remember this for a long time, all the brownies were gathered in the changing room and each had managed to change into their costumes among the hustle and bustle and frantic panic of the organizer's.

"Come on girls quiet now."

Team leader was shouting as she clapped her hands to distract the babbling youngsters, doing here best to get a team spirit we marched into the pool area and I was amazed at the size of the pool, it was the biggest thing I had ever seen, making brown owls pool resemble a bath in comparison.

Looking around at all the people seating on both sides of the pool I thought they must be very close to the clouds, scanning the crowds looking for my brothers and others from the home, but there were too many people.

"What do we have to do?" I nudged Tina sitting besides me.

"I don't know look at all the people, I am trying to see my mummy."

"Sit here girls and wait for your names to be called, we are the green team."

I looked all around in a state of wonderment, the sun cascaded through the large glass roof bouncing off the water that was the bluest of blues I had ever seen, making it appear like a tropical sea. I watched the small ripples dancing across the top of the water; skimming the surface and appeared to be chasing each other, softly disappearing into the walls of the pool only to start again. It reminded me of the beach I could hear nothing of the surrounding noise, and was totally lost in my own imagination; the whistle being blown interrupted my thoughts, the umpire informed the race was about to begin, I cheered my team mates on and even managed to pick Paul, and Mark, out from the crowds, they had made their way to the front of the isles.

Paul gave me his special wink, the one that told me all was fine.

"From the green team may we have." I listened to the loud speaker.

"Amy Wilkinson, Catherine Jones, Sharon Arscott, please take your places to start your race."

Making my way to the edge of the pool walking with pride and stature all eyes upon me, trying to get my swimming cap on, the elastic cap was hard it felt like a vice, pulling and tugging trying to tuck all my hair in.

I stood waiting, wondering why the others were not standing next to me, why was thick rope going up and down the pool and not across.

"Sharon this way" the team leader was ushering me to the starting point the crowd started to laugh; I blushed and stood where the team leader placed me.

"Ok girls gently ease yourselves into the water."

I did as told, the coldness took my breath away and also a little deeper than brown owl's pool, clinging onto the side seemed the best option.

"I may only have to do it once but it's going to take me forever." I thought as I looked straight ahead.

"On your Marks, get set, go." the starter shouted we were off.

I was bobbing my way towards the girls waiting at the other end, but some thing was not right I was finding it difficult some one had taken the floor away.

My bobbing was more of a jump, and the jumps were getting harder and harder, turning into a leap.

I was underneath the water watching the legs of my friends thrashing past, trouncing and spluttering I took in the water trying to scream, but every thing sounded muffled suddenly I felt myself being lifted out of the pool, the lifeguard had grabbed the straps of my costume and yanked me out.

Placing me on the side of the pool looking like a drowned rat, I was trying to release the costume from between my buttocks that had become tightly embedded, to this day I swear some one in the crowd saw this went away; and invented the first thong. I thought my lungs would burst as I coughed and spluttered, water coming out of my mouth, my eyes blood shocked from trying to see under the water. The guard wrapped me in a towel and immediately got me to the hospital where I was kept over night.

The doctor wanted to make sure I was fine before he discharged me home the following morning; he pulled me onto his lap and in a gentle voice said…

"Sharon my child the best advice I can give you is, hopping is for frogs swimming for fish, being a fish is more constructive when trying to get down stream." he winked as he left the room, I was taught to swim very soon after.

✤ CHAPTER THREE ✤

NO ONE CAME TO THE HOME TO ADOPT ANY OF us children people wanted babies, the few years that passed were uneventful we were good children and worked hard at school, and were academically average Paul, twelve Mark, eleven and I, a very serious nine years old, I was going to be ten in three months.

"Could you all go to the playroom?" Aunty Kay asked unexpectedly.

There was a special visitor to see us, as we entered the room a lady sat at the far wall looking harsh, her bright red lipstick standing out like a warning light emphasizing the thinness of her lips, she was of heavy build and not very tall, I stared opened mouthed transfixed on this person before me.

"Do you know who I am…. I am your mother."

Mark ran to her opened armed, but myself and Paul held back, I had seen Petula Clark on the television and was sure my mother resembled her, this stranger looked nothing like her. She was dressed all in black and looked very stern even though she were smiling, besides, if Paul was afraid then there was a good reason, he was never wrong.

After a lot of coaxing Paul and I moved closer, Mark, was already on her lap and curiosity overcame us, we were aching for our mother's love, all three willing to receive it unconditionally.

I kept checking making sure aunty Kay stayed in the room; she sat at the back watching how we integrated,

"Where have you been all this time?" Paul asked,

"Finding some where for all of us to live"

I was unsure about her, I wanted to trust but was afraid she would disappear again; the trauma of loosing another parent was too much to deal with.

"Would you like to go to the park next week? I will come and pick you up."

That sounded like fun, Paul looked to Aunty Kay for guidance before he would answer her, I was not bothered either way Mark, was more enthusiastic towards the treats she was promising.

"Would you like to see my toys?" Mark excitedly asked

"That would be nice" she held Marks hand as he led her towards the toy boxes. Her white stiletto heels clip clopped on the floor as she walked, and for a while all nerves were forgotten as each showed our favourite toys.

"Sharon, show your mother the car in the garden I am sure she would like that Mrs Davie, Is that ok with you?"

"Yes that's fine"

"Davie? You're not our mother." Paul accused

"You have the wrong name"

"She's not? How do you know?" Mark questioned.

"I am Paul; I just have a different name that's all"

Mother tried to explain to us bewildered children as I edged my way towards Paul, Mark was baffled not understanding what was happening, Aunty Kay explained as best she could,

"Take your mother into the garden Sharon, and Mark, I need to talk to Paul"

Again we both looked to Paul for encouragement, he winked but I was unsure. Initially telling me she is a fake mother, and then he tells me it's ok to go into the garden with her.

"We have chickens, geese and cockerels, and apples and pear trees, and the longest grass, I boasted.

"That's nice have you many friends?"

"Oh yes, lots of friends do you live down the road?"

"I used to but now I live in a place called Devon, I used to live in a village called Ebbw vale, not to far from here, why do you ask"

"When I was in the hospital a lady said you lived just down the road, but Paul said you were dead we were orphans"

"You are not orphans, and I am most certainly not dead"

There was a tone to her voice that made me a little fearful, we ambled towards the gates Paul, had rejoined us I held mothers hand skipping along side whilst Paul walked beside Aunty Kay.

The gate closed behind her and Mark asked if she would return

"Of course, she wants to get to know all her children trust her Mark, she will be back"

"Why now? Why after all this time, I don't trust her"

"Paul Come now every one deserves a second chance, she will be back"

Making our way back to the house I was getting excited about the next visit, time passed slowly and the night before she was due to arrive I was convinced she would not bother. Watching through the window the following morning willing for mother to appear at the gate, the front door bell could be heard all over the house.

"Some one has rang the bell come on Paul, it must be her."

I shouted excitedly whilst running down the stairs to answer the door,

"Where is Mark?"

"There he is."

Mark had been to the little boy's room hearing the doorbell he thought he was going to be left behind, and was still pulling his trousers up as he headed towards the door, both Paul and I laughed.

Walking to the park I had constantly dreamt this moment, played it over and over in my head the reality was not as exciting and emotional as the fantasy. Staying out for an hour Paul, was bored he was past the age of wanting to stay in the park, all of us including mother were feeling the strain of this visit, on returning home we ran into the house to watch our favourite programme on the television.

Remembering I had not said good-bye to mother I dashed back hoping to catch her before she left, approaching aunty Kay's private room I could hear mother's voice and decided to eavesdrop

"I don't know what is wrong with them but today was awkward I don't feel Paul is happy, and Sharon seems easily swayed by him."

"You have to give these children time Mrs Davie, they have been through a lot in their short lives, and you have been told about the last placement with the Beards? These things take time for children to get over."

Peeking through the crack in the door I noticed mother sitting on the sofa, she still had her scarf and coat on.

"Do you think they will ever be able to settle, we have been promised a house in Devon if the children are returned to me, the welfare will also supply their beds and various other things they will need"

"Just be patient all three want a family and I know how much Sharon has wanted this"

I was interrupted by Paul calling, Aunty Kay appeared at the door,

"What are you doing?"

"I wanted to say goodbye to mother, has she gone yet?"

Trying to sound surprised when told she had not.

"Come and say your goodbyes then."

I flung my arms around mother and tried to relax in her arms, but her touch was stiff and she seemed ill at ease with me, I watched as she left the house shaking off any doubts I ran back to the television room and placed myself next to my brothers.

It was decided that we were to go to mother's home in Devon for a week's trial, the summer holidays were starting next week. Boarding the train I was smiling so much my jaw was aching, all three of us were happy and it was our first time on a train, the countryside seemed to stretch forever in front of me, I loved the wonder of nature, all the seasons held a fascination, I never knew the world was so big every thing seemed greener and fresher, the hills rolling out ahead everything perfect. I studied my brother's faces looking for some clue to what they were thinking, Paul was looking out of the window he looked to me and winked his special wink.

Glancing over to Mark who sat on mothers lap, engrossed in what she was talking about, I was happy to be going home. At last the train pulled into our station, mother ordered us to hold onto her coat and not let go, no matter what happened. We were pushed and shoved as the people rushed to be first, I felt alarmed by the sheer volume of people. Pushing our way off the station and into the street seemed strange, I stood mesmerized by the sight before me never had I seen so much activity in one place. People beeping their car horns trying to get onto a busy road, buses parked at the designated stops ready to take every one home, the smell of the diesel over powering, the heat from the engines as a warm breeze.

We hurried to a big shinny red bus, Paul and Mark rushed up the stairs and sat on the front seat.

"This is great I want to drive a bus when I leave school." Paul thrilled,

"Look at all the people are they all going home?"

"Most are I expect" mother answered.

The bus filled very quickly some even standing holding onto the cold steel bars, I was swallowed up in a mass of legs and bums feeling as though I was buried, there was no air and no view for me to watch how I wish I were taller.

A man with a black cap and blazer made his way through the people taking money and turning a handle on the side of a black tinned meter, ping, another ping, he pushed his way through the crowd I was thrilled by his heroic deed, he walked with attitude and stamina as the bus swayed around the corners and bends of the road.

"Who is he?"

"He is the conductor you buy your ticket from him."

"I bet he has lots of money every one is giving him money"

I decided to marry a conductor when I grew up, they looked dashing in their uniform, the bus rumbled along its route at each stop people got off and the bus started to empty. I was able to see the city as we tumbled on to our destination, I was feeling tired from the day's events and could feel the angel with her sleepy dust.

"I can see ships!" Mark exclaimed

"Where"

They both stood at the window with their noses pressed against the glass straining to see, I was shaken by their shouting, out of the dream like state I had slipped into.

"That's Devonport dockyard, that's where your fathers ship is docked get ready our stop, lets go, hang on tightly"

The bus started to slow down the button was pressed, ding, ding, I hung on to the sides of the seats until my knuckles turned white, wishing I could reach the steel bars, the steps on the bus were steep, my legs straining made harder by the bus stopping and the people behind surging forwards as it slowed down, stepping off the bus I felt I would rather not have to go through that again, my brothers thought it was the best thing they had ever done.

Standing at the top of the street looking towards mother's home I was astounded, the houses were all joined together.

"Which one is ours?" Mark asked.

"We live in the middle every one stay on the pavement and carry your own bags; you are all old enough to do for your selves."

We approached the house through the back lanes mother was finding it difficult to walk on the small cobbles, removing her shoes she continued bare foot.

"We are in Coronation Street, the one on the television." Mark squealed with delight

"We are? Wow where does Hilda live?"

I enthralled, mother was laughing so hard she could only just catch her breath to explain we were wrong, again her mood had changed we were ushered into a gate and mother pronounced we were home.

An outside toilet was shown to us and explained it was the only one, I was a little uneasy it smelled strongly of urine and had cobwebs everywhere; it also had newspaper cut into squares and hung on string. Mark peeked inside when he saw me screwing up my nose; he asked mother why the paper was there

"You use it for bog roll."

"Bog rolls what's bog roll?"

"Bloody hell… toilet roll"

I put my hand over my own mouth and giggled

"That's a naughty word."

Paul and Mark fell about laughing pushing each other and fooling around mimicking mother, and her words of bog roll.

"Oh for Christ sake Sharon come down off your fucking high horse." she snapped.

Silence fell between all we were trying to decipher what the new words and phrases meant, accent and values were very different here and mother knew quite a few swear words. The house was small, two rooms down and two up; it was sparsely furnished and dark and dreary.

"Where is the bathroom?" Mark inquired,

"There is no bathroom."

"Then how do we wash? Or bathe?"

"In the steel tub in that cupboard"

Mother dragged out a large tin bucket and went on to explain the procedure of filling and emptying it, I had never seen a house like this it was going to take some getting used to for all of us, space was some thing we had in abundance, we found some toys in the shed at the back of the house.

"Put them back they are not yours."

mother was agitated by us touching the toys the first few days were strained as we all tried to get to know each other, we stayed close to the house although we were allowed to play on the street, neither of us wanted to, Paul was getting agitated with Mark he was happy to wonder off, further than Paul thought was safe.

I would walk a little way from the house but turn back for fear of getting lost, all the houses looked the same and I had gone into the wrong house a few times making the owners angry.

"There is not a lot to do here." Mark moaned as he doodled on the pavement with a stick, the sun was beating down, the air sticky; we had spent three days hanging around the house. Mother watched television and smoked a lot, we were starting to miss home thing's were different here.

We slept together in mother's bed; mother was sleeping on the sofa.

"What about the other room? Why don't you sleep there?" Paul asked

"It is June's room and I have promised her no one will go in it"

"Who is June?"

"I will tell you later stop asking so many bloody questions." she snapped

I found some things mother said odd, some times I wanted to ask questions about some of the answers she gave, but decided to leave well alone.

Mother made me feel uneasy at times, and would have an odd look in her eye or maybe answer a little sharply, and then cover it over pretending it was a joke.

Mother explained father was in the navy and he would be visiting in a few days, we also had a younger sister who was staying with grandparents, so the mystery of June was solved.

"Cant make head nor tail about mother, one minute she says don't ask who June is, then she tells me." Paul was shaking his head mother's moods were worrying, when ever any one asked about June, she became defensive, if we touched her toys we were told to leave them alone. This was strange to us we never had our own toy box, I sneaked into her bedroom to see what it was like, there were so many toys I could not believe they all belonged to one person, I felt a little envious of this sister called June.

I hurried back down to join every one in the kitchen and heard Mark explaining to mother he was bored,

"We will see what the weather is like tomorrow if it is fine we shall go to the beach"

"The one we passed on the bus the other day?" Mark added fidgeting with excitement.

"No that was a Dockyard this is another place,"

"Brilliant" I chirped up, "I am going to bed early so tomorrow will come quicker."

"Christ almighty girl you have bloody big ears do you always listen to people's conversations?"

There was an element of spite in the way she spoke, I stood rigid not sure how to react; it was another one of those confused situations.

"Only joking, don't be so bloody serious you don't like me do you?"

Mother drew heavy on yet another cigarette the stench from her breath unpleasant.

"I do, I umm I need to go to the toilet" I lied wanting to get out of the room not knowing how to react to her mood.

I went to bed early to stay out of her way, I felt mother may not like me very much I will try harder tomorrow. All my wishes were coming true a family of our own this was our real family; I desperately wanted it to work.

The morning sun shone bright through our bedroom window,

making the room feel warm jumping out of bed I threw back the curtains shouting to my brothers to get up quick, today we were off to the beach. Mother was in the kitchen and explained we had to leave straight away, we had slept late this morning and if we did not hurry we would have no where to sit. We walked along talking about school and our friend's, mother seemed interested in what we had to say.

"Why are we walking, why don't we have a mini bus?"

"God gave you legs to walk, fucking use them" was her reply, I studied her as she lit a cigarette and drew heavy onto it the smoke oozing from her nostrils, I imagined her as a dragon and quickly averted my stare as her eyes bore into mine, I decided to walk a little behind.

"Just around this corner not far now," mother reassured sensing that the walk was getting a little long and boring.

"This is a big hill we don't have many hills at home, here they are every where" Paul joked,

The sea breeze was cooling on my face, I could smell the salt water as we approached the promenade, and standing on the grass looking at the view of the landscape, the small inlets and coves visible from my perch seemed to keep the sea at bay.

Fishing boats and sailboats filled the sea before me the sailboats glided over the sea as a skater on ice, the gulls shadowing the fishing boats as they sailed into port, diving into the sea as the crew threw the offal from the days catch. It appeared to be a very busy place there was a lot of activity, glancing around people sat on the grass in small groups every one seemed relaxed and enjoying the fine summer weather.

This has to be the best place I have ever seen,

"Why are there so many boats?"

"Devon has many fishing ports all around the coast we have small inlets, and one day I will take you around to the different ones" she promised.

Look, a swimming pool and diving boards, look, even boats"

Paul was running around pointing out every thing, we were all amazed the only beaches we had seen were sand and sea with caravans; I looked to see where the caravans were placed in this adventurous wonderland.

"Let's ask mother if we can go to the pool"

"Come on then we have all day," mother replied

Words failed me how happy I felt it was a nice feeling just to be able to say

"LET'S ASK MOTHER"

Mother took me to the changing rooms explaining she would meet me outside, I protested, afraid of being left alone but she was adamant and a little harsh as she explained I was a big girl and I needed to be more independent, I wanted to ask what independent meant, but was afraid she may leave me.

When I had dressed and went to meet them I could not find them, searching up and down it seemed like a long time I decided to walk around for a while, there was so much going on around here it reminded me of the holidays taken by the sea. Up and down I walked stopping for a while and watching people diving off a large diving board, wishing I could do it. From the promenade I had a good view of the beach and surrounding areas, once more walking slowly straining to see mother, time was moving on I started to get upset, this was the longest time I had been alone. I thought mother had left me and wished I had asked what dependant meant, a passer-by asked what was wrong and I explained I was lost, she took me to the nearest police station.

The police informed the lost and found unit and they spoke on the load speaker with my details, I sat in a small office feeling lost and dejected, the officer asked if I would like a drink his moustache reminded me of a man from my past whom I had loved very much, and missed. Invoking memories of the first time I met father Beard.

We were gathered in the playroom of the toddler's home I had lived for two months, eleven thirty that morning a couple arrived we were all excited at the prospect of a new mummy and daddy, Mark was inquisitive and circled round the couple at a safe distance. Curiosity got the better of me, peeking through the crowd of youngsters I wanted to see what a real mummy and daddy looked like.

It amused me that they look like any other man or woman; the lady looked kind her long flowing black hair swung around her face as she tried to answer all the inquisitive questions from the little ones. A younger child sat on her knee lapping up the attention she was receiving, I envied her.

"Hello, what's your name?"

I shied away back into the gathering of excited children, desperately wanting to be held the same way, but afraid of being picked and separated from my brothers. The man looked sterner but strong and dashing; he winked at me and gave a little wave, once again I shyly disappeared to the back of the group but this time he followed.

"Hello, would you like to show me some toy's I don't have any toy's at home."

I felt a little threatened by his presence and wasn't sure about the hair on his lip, I thought it looked a little like the rat in my books.

"You're not afraid of me surly, come on darling I don't bite, what's your name"

"Sharon."

"That's a pretty name for a very pretty girl; would you like to show me around?"

"Um no…I need to stay here I am playing with Molly, she's my best friend"

Molly appeared by my side.

"Hello Molly, so you are Sharon's best friend? My you are a pretty little thing so many pretty little girls here" Molly gave him her best smile.

"I surely am her best friend mister, we play together all the time, don't we Sharon"

I nodded in agreement to what ever Molly had to say, Molly was the more out going and nearly seven years old three years older than I.

"You are wanting for a girl mister, or a boy?" Molly inquired pulling her socks up in an uneasy manner,

"Oh I think maybe a little girl would you like a mummy and daddy darling?" he turned and asked me.

"No, she doesn't need any new mummy and daddy mister she stays here with her brothers and me,"

Molly answered defiantly.

"Oh I see, and what do you think darling"

"I think my brother wants me over there."

I whispered pointing to Paul, who had ushered me over towards him; Molly had already gone distracted by the juice and cakes that had been bought into the playroom.

"Ok darling off you go would you like us to come and see you again?"

"If you want to"

I skipped off to re-join Molly and my brothers, taking one last sneaky look back at the man, I liked him.

When they had gone things returned to normal.

"You should have gone and seen the new mummy and daddy perhaps they would want you Molly, and they are looking for a girl"

"I don't need a new momma I already have one she is just lost is all, and she is coming to get me soon"

I was intrigued,

"Why did she get lost? How are you going to find her?"

I asked while trying to undress my doll.

"Shoot, I surely don't know how but she did, she did not come home from the shop we came all the way to England on a boat and she gets lost going shopping"

Molly was engrossed in the dressing of her doll.

"You came here on a boat? I came in a car you are lucky Molly"

I was always eager to listen to Molly's stories about a land far, far away, where the sun shines all year and the mud like sand.

"How will she know how to find you if you are not at home, will she need the boat to go shopping as well?"

"Oh! I left a note, Michael helped me to write it cause I don't spell to well, A BOAT? You silly" Molly teased,

"Some times you funny, what about your mummy? Is she lost too?"

"I don't think so Paul said she's dead, and my daddy but I don't think that means lost, I know she is not in Africa, because I came from another house like this one"

I answered thinking deeply about the true meaning of dead.

"There I did it look," I squealed with delight,

"I dressed my dolly all by myself."

The conversation regarding lost parents were soon forgotten,

I had reached a milestone in my young life, dressing dolly all by myself.

It had been a few weeks since the special visitors had come and a distant memory to the little ones. Spring was in the air the weather was starting to get warmer, and only five more weeks before I started my first day at infant's school.

"Why are my good clothes on my bed?" I asked my nurse "Are more people coming for a reject?"

"Reject, Sharon! What ever do you mean darling?" the nurse asked horrified.

"Mark says we are all rejects of life and we have to wait and see if others want a reject, but I don't know what a reject is, and Mark wont tell me either"

"Come here and sit for a while we need to talk"

Patting the bed the nurse indicating for me to sit,

I was a little worried what I said was wrong,

"Honey you are not a reject you are a beautiful little girl, I would be proud to have you as my daughter" she soothed gently stroking my hair.

"I don't mind I know we are not really because Paul told me we are organs,"

I was getting very serious with my answers trying to remember exactly what Paul had told me.

"Organs?" the nurse laughed, trying hard not to make me feel inadequate with my interpretation.

"What's funny? Is an organ funny" screwing up my nose glad I made the nurse smile.

"I am not sure darling but you really are a prize and if you are picked to go to a new family it's because you are special, you must always remember that."

The nurse hugged me tightly making me feel secure, I loved this sort of attention some one knocking on my bedroom door distracted me,

"Come in"

"Sharon you ready to play down stairs?" Mark asked,

The nurse butted in before I could answer,

"Where's Paul poppet?"

"I am here," he piped up popping his head around the door.

"Paul darling what's Sharon mean when she says you are all organs?"

"Organs Sharon, what are you going on about now? I don't know what she means," Paul scolded.

"Yes you do, Mark says we are rejects, and you said no we are organs, when I asked where mummy and daddy were" I started to get frustrated fearing no one understood what I meant, at four years old it is some times hard.

"Organs" both Mark and Paul started to tease

"You play music with an organ, I said orphans, you silly" they continued to mock.

"Ok boys she's only little and got a little mixed with her words."

The nurse added trying to hide my obvious annoyance.

"Down stairs boys, Sharon will be along soon"

She clapped her hands trying to distract them from their laughter; they could still be heard laughing as they descended the stairs, I stood totally puzzled by the behaviour of my brothers,

"They are being silly," I scorned, "they always tease me."

"Never mind, come on we will get you dressed."

"What for?"

"You are going into town for the day with Mark and Paul, and some special people."

"Oh thank you I am going to tell Molly."

Rushing down the stairs and into the playroom I did not hear my nurse calling.

"Molly, guess what? I am going into town with some special people."

"Can I come, can we bring the dollies and the prams, and we can go to a park."

Molly was getting enthralled in the coming trip, rushing back up the stars to my bedroom the nurse was making the beds.

"Can Molly come as well? Can we take the prams?"

"Sharon slow down."

The nurse explained only me and my brothers were invited, we waited in the sitting room all dressed clean and neat, Molly poked her head around the door,

"I aint allowed to go with you."

"Molly, come out side and play"

She was ushered away before I could answer.

"It's that man who has eaten a rat." I informed my nurse as I hid behind her.

"Sharon! That's very rude what ever has got into you?"

"I am not going I don't like him"

The nurse lifted me onto her lap and the Lady and man were asked to wait in another room.

"Come on darling what's wrong?" the nurse tried to coax, "They are very nice people and they like you a lot"

"He has swallowed a rat I can see the tail on his lip" I buried my head into the chest of the nurse not wanting to look at any one.

"Sharon poppet" the nurse trying not to laugh out loud,

"It's called a moustache lots of men have them and one day maybe even Paul and Mark will,"

"Come on they won't hurt us I will look after you, people don't eat animal's any way." Mark was getting a little agitated in case the couple left.

"They do too, Molly told me about Africa."

"Now children please calm down Mark, please be quiet, Sharon, you are right about Africa, and I know how confusing things can be."

The nurse tried her best to explain things but I was already a very frightened and confused little girl.

After a lot of talking and explaining I Agreed to go into town with the couple, we were told we did not have to do any thing that felt uneasy. I was not sure what uneasy felt like, and was confused with many expressions the grown ups used.

It also made my nurses aware of how shielded our lives in the orphanage were, very little contact with adult males were to be made most staff apart from the gardener, were female and almost all the males were of the same young age as I. But my life was to change and my fist day at infant's school attended with my own mummy and daddy at my side.

Mother eventually turned up to collect me four hours later snapping me out of my reverie of distant memories.

"Thank you so much for finding her she wondered off, I hope she has been no trouble" mother was very flustered.

"She was an absolute delight no trouble what's so ever" the officer replied ruffling my hair.

"We have been looking for her all this time these dear boys have not been able to have a swim, that was very naughty of you Sharon" mother scolded.

"We have rung the welfare the kid has been here four hours and did not know her address, she kept saying she lived a long train journey away, we put her details out on the loud speakers, we thought she was a tourist"

"Oh we did not hear the announcement until about five o'clock, we walked all the way home to make sure she had not gone back, oh well I must go thank you once again"

We left the police station and started the long tiring walk home.

"Don't you ever do that again young lady?" mother shouted walking faster and dragging me along, gripping my hand tightly, mother hissed father was home tonight and I was to be punished for getting lost, I started to cry as mother explained that he was not our real father, only Junes, but we were lucky to have him this confused the hell out of me.

"Where is my real daddy?" I asked.

He does not want any of you,"

Her pace getting faster as she spoke I was running to keep up with her.

"He was the one who took you away from me and dumped you in the children's orphanage; Taffy will be dad from now on"

She was rambling, something in her voice told us to drop the subject, glancing up at mothers face her features seemed harder the breath from her nostrils like the ones from the angry bull facing the matador, things were about to take a dramatic turn.

"Will we be meeting our grandparents?"

"You have no grandparents Sharon"

"We do, they bought us a watch and we write to them, don't we Paul"

"No you bloody well don't they won't be writing any more it was me who sent you the watches,"

We glanced at each other quickly screwing our faces, Paul shrugged his shoulders, but neither of us argued with her the rest of the journey was walked in silence. Eventually arriving home mother's mood became more unpredictable, she was angry with me and threatened me again with step-father. I was becoming more and more afraid.

"We will hide you," Paul reassured

"We can hide you behind the television."

I hoped they where right.

"When are we going to eat mother we are hungry" Paul inquired

"You had lunch late so you can wait for tea until your father gets here, he will arrive about eight o'clock"

Paul was unsure whether to reply in case she was a little confused with the day's events.

"But we have not eaten today we have had nothing"

"Don't talk such rubbish of course you have eaten you had toast for breakfast, and fish and chips for lunch, Jesus you bloody kids you must have hollow legs"

Turning her back on Paul and lighting another cigarette he was confused, Mark and I were listening at the door we hurried back to the lounge and watched as Paul entered, rubbing his head in deep thought.

"Have we eaten today?"

"No we have not,"

"It is so much different here do you know we have not had a bath since we came here, or cleaned our teeth" I mussed.

"Yes bloody great isn't it" Mark added we started to laugh settling to watch the television, mother stayed in the kitchen alone.

We heard a deep voice talking to mother, she was shouting about the day's events my name was mentioned over and over, her words damming for the inconvenience I had caused.

"I think it must be dad," Mark worried.

My brothers hid me as promised, the lounge door opened and I watched as a foot appeared in the room, it looked more like a shovel my heart beating fast I thought it would pop from my chest.

"Where's your sister?" he boomed.

"Behind the television," they answered in unison; guess they had the same opinion of him, he bent down to lift me up

"Heard you got lost today and frightened your mother"

He was big and strong yet gentle, I liked him straight away, he played games with us and was interested in every thing we had to say. The evening went well, although mother did not join in preferring to stay in the kitchen, step-father cooked supper and explained he would have to leave very soon to go back on ship.

After he left mother informed us it was time for bed, we climbed the stairs excited chit chat about stepfather's visit rang through the house, mother started to shout at me for getting lost earlier in the day.

Pulling my hair things were happening to quick for me to react, mother forced my face down onto the rough carpet and started dragging me down the stairs, Paul and Mark were horrified, I was in shock. With clenched fist she was punching my stomach Paul lifted his foot and kicked out at mother causing her to fall down the remaining stairs. He was sure I was going to die if he did not respond.

We ran as fast as our legs would carry us into the bedroom horrified, I was sobbing.

"I want to go home,"

Mark was worried mother was dead, she had not returned upstairs, Paul was trying to be brave telling me he would not let anyone else hurt me, a fact he was not so sure if mother had gone to fetch step-father.

"Let's run away I want to go on the train I want to go home" I kept repeating.

"We can't go any where we would have to go down stairs she maybe waiting."

Paul was trying desperately to hide his fears, Mark was silently crying torn between wanting to protect me, and wanting to make sure mother was fine.

"Let's climb out of the window then we can run back to the beach, find that police station"

I was getting desperate to find ways to get out of the house.

"Sharon we can't go out we don't know our way around let's get into bed and try and sleep, she hasn't come back, what do you think Mark?"

"I think we are in deep trouble and will be on stair duty for a week when we get home, Sharon what did you do to her?"

I was puzzled what had I in fact done to cause this reaction.

"I don't know maybe because I spoiled your day when I got lost,"

"No, it cant be that because we went to the swimming pool we had a great time, we knew where to find you because it came over the load speaker, mother told us to enjoy ourselves that you would turn up like a bad sixpence" Mark explained.

"A bad penny, not sixpence" Paul corrected

"Get into bed; here sleep in the middle, that way she won't get you"

I scurried quickly between my brothers, most of the night I lay awake listening for a clue to what mother was doing, eventually falling asleep, I was desperate to return home this had happened in the other family when I was thrown naked in the nettles, I turned over and buried my head into my pillow crying silently not wanting to be heard for fear of mothers return.

Mother calling us downstairs for breakfast woke us I did not want to go down, and would rather stay for ever in this small room, taking my time to dress. Gingerly making our way down stairs making sure I was last

"Morning what would you like to eat for breakfast?"

Mother greeted us with a smile and a hug; it was as though last night never happened I were grateful to her, although I did not understand what I had done but was happy she was happy, and that she may love me again.

One day left until we were due to return to Wales I was excited, afraid of mother her behaviour confusing we stayed at the house and mother played games with us, I started to believe I may have dreamt the events of yesterday. Returning home I re-iterated my reservations to Aunty Kay, but mother gave a different version and convinced them I was over reacting, the powers that be decided we would be returned permanently to mother. When we were informed Mark was happy, Paul wanted desperately to belong and was hoping for it to work I was scared, I knew not of what, but felt insecure with mother, talking to Aunty Kay she convinced me it was perfectly normal to have these doubts besides, it was my real mother she would not allow anything to happen to either of us.

No one could possible conceived the devastation and abuse all three of us would experience in the next five years.

⇥ Chapter Four ⇤

After a few weeks we packed our bags and headed once again to the train station, this time accompanied by one of the aunties from the home.

"Your mother will meet your train,"

"Will you be coming to the house with us?"

"Of course silly I will make sure that and your brothers are settled besides; I have to wait for the next train back to Wales"

Boarding the train for the final journey home the enthusiasm of our first trip had disappeared, it was possibly the quietest journeys we were ever going to make.

Aunty was trying to muster up some enthusiasm from us, as we exited the train I could see mother on the platform Mark ran to her.

"Hello I am Jean, I have travelled down with the children you must be very excited I know the children are, and it's all they have talked about." she lied.

"Come on lets get every one in the taxi and home we have a new house with three bedrooms and a bathroom, just for you kids."

This excited me and grabbed our attention, no outside toilet and sharing a bed with my brothers, the taxi drew up out side a house on a hill it looked ok, the front door was open and a young girl waved excitedly.

"Who's that?"

"That is June, your baby sister"

This angered me I felt pangs of jealousy towards her, dropping our bags onto the hallway floor we proceeded to the lounge. A lady was sitting on the sofa and introduced herself as a neighbour, she had sat with June whilst mother met us, mother thanked her and she left.

The furnishings were better than the other house June wanted to show me our bedroom, giving a guided tour enthusiastically she showed me the boy's bunk beds their room was small, there was a very narrow landing with a large cupboard.

"This is mum and dad's room"

They had a double bed and wardrobe it looked neat and tidy, ours was next door it had two beds and no other furnishings.

Which bed would you like? Take your pick"

I chose the bed behind the door maybe having a little sister won't be so bad after all, she seems nice. Skipping excitedly out of the room June wanted to show me her toys.

"I don't think I have seen so many toys that belonged to one person" Jean commented.

"We don't have any toys" Paul was trying to explain to June,

"No toys? Why not, every one has toys what about Father Christmas; he must have bought you toys?"

"You can play with Junes toys" mother butted in.

We were a little apprehensive remembering mother's attitude the last time we dare to play.

I introduced Molly Dolly to June, and explained she was special, even though I were too old to play with her and the memory of Molly fading, the doll was all I had left.

"I should be going my train is due soon"

"Come and wave me off"

Aunty climbed into the taxi and we waved her off I looked around the street and noticed other children watching, I hurried into the safety of the house and was sure everything was going to be ok. Mark was starting his first year in secondary education, a big change for him, he was nearly twelve years old, and I and June were to attend the local junior school. I was amazed June was only eighteen months younger than I, it soon became apparent to the three of us that mother had more love for her.

We were excluded from most things and a paper round waiting for us when we first arrived from the orphanage, handing our wages over to mother to pay towards our food the explanation given for such a charge, our real father wont pay towards food and clothes, so we have to.

Step-Father was away at sea for the first few months and we were learning to avoid mother and her moods swings which could be violent and mostly aimed at me.

Saturday was a day I learned to despise, each week we were promise a late nights feast, each week the same ritual the longing to be included, this was a practice I began to loathe. In my bed awake smelling the odours of the treat mother was cooking sometimes if I had not eaten for a few days I could taste the odours that filtered through the house.

"I won't give you any dinner," mother would explain to all "there will be plenty to eat later, now off to bed all of you and I will call you down later."

Every Saturday evening I would tip-toe down the stairs hoping to be allowed to join in. The first few times I was convinced mother had forgotten me, but after being beaten for daring to ask to be included I decided not to ask any more, knowing my attempts were futile. Sitting with my beloved Molly Dolly, alone in my room sadness engulfed me like a shawl I was terribly lonely. The following morning mother informed me she had waited for me to attend and I had only myself to blame for falling asleep. I cried for three hours, the pain of hunger twisting my belly like a rag squeezed of water. The weekly ritual of pleas to be included resumed, afraid to stop asking in case this was my lucky night.

Each week the rejection each week the silent tears into my pillow, I longed to be loved! How eager I was to please as time went by I stopped asking but got wise, if I woke before mother I was able to eat the scraps left on their plates, mother also got wise and would deliberately leave the waste in the bin, disposing the contents of her ashtrays on top. Hunger knows no dignity and I would take whatever I could and devour it like a banquet.

There was also a void developing between my siblings and I, we were learning to survive to look after him or her self. We accepted the things that went on and soon it became a way of life, we had no one to turn to for help. Curiosity about my biological father was mounting I wanted to know his name, where he lived, what sort of person he was. The only one able to answer questions was mother, to ask her would result in a flurry of blows, timing must be right or just leave it until I was older, the latter seemed the better option.

I constantly tried to be a good girl, when entering the home I felt as though I were entering a dark damp cave and the beast was ready to devour my very soul. Studying my reflection in the mirror, mother's words swirling round my head,

"You ugly fat cow and, you aren't a virgin the backs of your legs are flat, you will always be second best to your sister."

Step-Father was soon due home for good things were always easier when he was around mother's moods were calmer. School holidays were starting next week and step-father was home permanently; mother had started work and step-father looked after us we were more at ease with him.

The first day of the summer holidays and nothing was mentioned about going away, Mother announced she was off for two weeks to visit Granny, and June was going with her. I often wondered why mother never referred to Granny being ours, we were upset with the arrangement but none would dare voice their opinion.

Mark was upset father had started to bully him, mother was protective of him and would not allow this to happen, Paul on the other hand did not have the same protection from her, nor I. We were also upset by the rejection of mother's family never having met our grandparents, aunties or uncles. I was relieved, at least for two weeks I would be treated the same as my brothers and fed, my belly rumbled and squeaked as hunger danced her tune.

Step-father beat all of us but never starved me, he always made sure there was plenty food for all, the days tumbled by in a quite haze of peace and calm, mother was due home in seven days and I dreaded it, I wanted things to stay as they were. Step-father had been calmer although we all tried harder to stay out of his way, especially when he arrived home drunk.

He announced a new carpet was to be laid as a surprise for mother on her return, we set about helping him he ordered me to crawl underneath and straighten the newspaper that was used as underlay, I was eager to please. As I forced my way under the carpet I felt someone touch me between my legs, turning instantly to see who had done this. Horrified to witness it was step-father, instantly I confronted him he denied it, neither of my brothers would admit to witnessing it. What had I done to make him do that? He became more aggressive towards me as the days went by, returning home drunk and making excuses to beat me he was becoming a drunken bully who seemed to enjoy the power he had over us.

My brothers and I were sat in the lounge watching the television, mother was due home tomorrow and we knew we had to leave the house before step-father returned from the pub. We had got engrossed by the program time was ticking away faster than either had anticipated. The back door was slammed shut looking towards each other searching for answers, the lounge door flew open step-father placed a shoe against it to keep it from closing.

"Three sneaky Fucking bastards watching the television" he sneered. He was drunk and in a foul mood my mind raced through different scenarios of escape.

He went back to the kitchen and emptied his pockets of stolen food he regularly obtained, shoplifting gave him more money for cider, he was damned good at it his pockets had been made larger to accommodate his trade. He started to chop a large joint of meat with an axe he kept in the kitchen.

"Who's going to peel the spuds for chips," he bellowed.

"You go" Paul whispered to Mark

"No you".

"Sharon go on you go, he wont hit you" Mark said almost pleading.

"No not me"

The decision taken from us when he re-appeared and scowled

"Get here bitch, peel the spuds"

I moved into the kitchen, the thought crossed my mind to make a mad dash out the back door, but I talked myself out of it, nervously peeling the spuds that had been thrown into the sink trying to make conversation keeping him sweet.

"Did you have a good time at the pub Dad?"

"What's it to do with you bitch? One day I will sell you to my friends, you will make me money"

Brushing him self against me I felt uneasy, the mood in the kitchen not right I tried to move slightly to the left he slapped me on the side of my face,

"Look at the thickness of the peelings bitch I could make bloody chips from them"

"Sorry dad, I won't do it again"

But I was more upset by his actions feeling unsafe in a different way, I didn't like the way he brushed against me.

"Finished, I will clean up and then can I go out?"

Trying to sound as though I was not worried about anything,

"No, go back into the lounge I will cook your dinner make sure you don't bloody lie about not eating" he mocked.

Pressing his body into mine pretending little room was available for him to pass, grabbing both my arms he pinned them down to my sides. His breathing heavy he was wiping his face in my hair, his breathing getting deeper his breathe foul-smelling of stale ale.

"You know you want me,"

He whispered in my ear, I started to get scared and pull away in a manner that did not show my terror,

"I umm, I umm I've finished"

frightened to sound to upset for fear of provoking him into doing some thing; I wanted to be in view of my brothers releasing his grip I slowly walked out of the kitchen sensing him leering at me as I exited the room.

Entered the living room I could see how agitated my brothers were, they sat on the edge of their seats hands clasped tightly on their knees whispering as low as I could I pleaded with them,

"Don't leave me here alone with him, no matter what happens"

"What?"

Both boys were studying my mouth trying to make sense of what I had said.

"DON'T LEAVE ME HERE ON MY OWN" I whispered in a clear tone.

We could hear the chopper connecting with the meat as he pounded it; he again appeared in the room.

"What you little bastards been doing today"

Throwing the chopper straight at Paul it stuck fast into the wall, Mark was shaking so hard he looked as though he were convulsing. Paul looked to me gesturing with his eyes, mouthing silently

"Where is he?" total terror coursed through us as we pulled and tugged at each other to hide.

Step-fathers rosy cheeks and slightly blue tipped nose told us he had his fair share of booze for the day; once again he returned to the kitchen and proceeded to open a tin of peas with the electric opener. Suddenly there was a loud bang and the television ceased to work, the house had a strange silence as we waited for his onslaught of anger, there was an almighty crash followed by a loud thud, we looked to each other every thing had gone quiet,

"Sharon go see"

"Not bloody likely, you go"

"We should all go" Mark whispered, peering into the kitchen I could see step-father's feet; his toes were facing towards the ceiling I knew instantly he was in trouble.

"Oh my god he's dead"

I placed my hand over my mouth as though it was a terrible thing to say, Paul urged me to go and have a proper look

"I am not going alone"

I was determined with this decision, cautiously we walked into the kitchen holding onto each other's clothing, I noticed the cord from the tin opener was burnt, the plug had been forced out of the plug socket, and peas littered the kitchen even on step-fathers face; Paul kicked his leg making sure there was no movement.

"He's dead bloody hell, nasty ass bastard"

Mark again nudged the leg and started to do a little jig.

"He's dead, he's dead"

Both Paul and Mark were singing this over and over I joined in, we were starting to get very loud, laughing, jumping around, and singing we became hysterical as relief swept over us. Stopping my little jig I concentrating on his face

"What's wrong now?"

"He moved I think, Paul I swear he moved"

"Nope Sharon the bastards definitely dead he wont ever be hitting any of us again"

I looked again realizing I was being silly re-joining the celebrations, some thing caught my eye I looked at step-father's face; my brothers were still dancing and kicking up a storm.

"There I knew it,"

Step-Father opened his eyes and looked right at me, he winked, grabbing Marks shirt I WAS tugging at it, no words could I find.

"What's wrong now, you look as though you have seen a ghost?"

All I could do was point; he was listening and taking in every thing, Mark gawked at step-father totally disbelieving what he was seeing pulling at Paul's jumper, step-father started to rise off the floor, Mark made a dash for the back door. he grabbed Marks leg tripping him up and pulling him back. We all started to cry; I did not want this to be happening

"So this is what you little bastards think of me, I put food in your bellies and the clothes on your back, what you do for me, dance around hoping I am dead."

The three of us started to run scatter like seeds in the wind, each hoping the other will be caught, blaming each other.

"It was him he made me do it" I chanted as his fists connected with my body.

"It was Sharon she made me do it"

Chanted Mark

"It was them, they said you were dead" Terrified Paul was screaming as the blows became unbearable, we rushed to our bedrooms pulling and grappling with each other hoping not to be the last up the stairs, whilst he reigned the blows down on us.

In our bedrooms we had time to reflect it had been a good hour since we had ran for our lives, Paul whispered to me

"Sharon you awake?"

"Yes why?"

"Come in here with us, he's asleep on the sofa he wont hear you"

"Like the last time Paul, like you said he was dead," I replied sarcastically

"Come on Sharon come in here with us" Mark pleaded.

I was still sobbing as I made my way, both sat on the top bunk Paul's face had carpet burns from being dragged; Marks injuries were hidden on the legs, I had a black eye and swollen wrist and bruising to my thigh, although the black eye was caused by my brothers as we wrestled up the stairs, one of them had elbowed me in their panic.

"Jesus what a bloody mess I think the bastard was awake all along, he tricked us"

"What would have happened if he had been dead?" Mark queried

"We would have been placed back into care I suppose"

The room fell silent as each of us remembered a life without fear, back in Wales.

"I truly wish he had died I hate him, and I would love to go back into an orphanage"

"Don't Sharon don't become bitter one day they will get their comeuppance."

Mark and Paul started to laugh at the way each had handled the situation,

"It's not funny you know look at the state of us"

"I know Sharon but you should have seen your face when he opened his eyes"

Mark laughed trying to keep his laughter low, I started to giggle,

"You should have seen you two"

"It's not funny really, shush"

I was trying to be serious but all of us were getting hysterical with laughter, we were petrified he would wake but could not stop; we had tears of laughter streaming down our cheeks.

"What about you cowards you yanked me down the stairs and then stood on me"

Paul added laughing quite hard.

"Shit, I was not about to be last I was afraid the bastard was going to come behind us on the bloody stairs, and kick the proverbial out of us" Mark shrieked. We stayed in our rooms until the next day talking about days gone by, and making a joke about resent events, I wanted to tell them what had transpired in the kitchen but was not exactly sure what had happened, only that I was starting to fear step-father in another way, and I was unsure about being left alone with him.

Through all our adversities we could still laugh, we kids had a hidden strength although we were led to believe we were nothing and worth less, we had a determination to survive, this was to hold all of us in good stead.

As soon as mother returned I told her what had happened how he touched me, he denied it. Mother asked the boys, they could not, or would not confirm it. I was waiting in my bedroom believing mother would sort it out, raised voices could be heard downstairs then I heard someone coming up the stairs; it was step-father.

"Why have you lied? What would you want to tell lies like that for?"

I was confused by this line of questioning opening my mouth to explain but nothing come out, my throat was dry I could feel the blood rushing to my head, my mind racing searching what to say, I was going to be in real trouble.

"Because your fucking mother went away you say these things about me? You lying bitch."

Grabbing my hair he forced my head towards the ground, I knew not to fight back.

"I'm sorry," I pleaded, Mother appeared in the room my heart lifted she would stop this; I looked up towards her pleading with my eyes to stop this onslaught. Bang! Blood was pouring from my nose, mother had punched me in the face step-father let go his grip and I sank to the floor mother was kicking me I was at their mercy; step-father jumped in and pulled her away.

"Stop, Jesus Christ you will kill her"

Mother was dragged from my bedroom kicking and screaming she had not finished with the little bitch yet, hours passed and no one came to my room, eventually mother appeared in the doorway, seizing my hair pulling her face level with my own I had never felt this scared,

"If you ever repeat lies like that again I will kill you" she spat.

"DO YOU UNDERSTAND ME BITCH?"

"Yes, yes, sorry mother, sorry"

I was trying to hide my tears I knew from past attacks crying or showing emotion only made the beating worse.

"Get downstairs and apologize to him"

I ran as fast as I could down the stairs certain mother would kick me down them if she were close behind, head down knowing not to make eye contact I apologized.

"It's OK but next time I will kill you, go and wash your face you're a disgrace"

I wanted to scream at him you bloody liar, but felt something inside slipping away it was hopeless; there was no one to help me from now on I had to survive, and be vigilant. How could mother not believe me I cried myself to sleep that night and felt the snowstorm in my heart, I was becoming cold unemotional and switching off, at eleven years of age my innocence was being snatched from me, by the very people I should be able to turn to. I never thought mother would disbelieve me I trusted her to protect me. After this I always referred to mother's husband as step-father, because no man should do to their daughter what this animal had done to me.

My only hope was to find my real father if I knew where he lived he would help, I could tell him what was going on he could put a stop to it, this thought was all that kept me going through the pain and heartache I was to endure.

After this the sexual abuse increased, at night when the house was still he would come to my room and use my body for his own perverted lust, never reacting to him deciding to detach myself from the unhealthy acts the depraved night devil bestowed upon me. I took my mind and soul to the beach at every opportunity, watching a storm the coarseness of the waves as they pounded the rocks, and the savage tide grasped the shore line pulling at the sand forcibly taking it back down into the jaws of the white frothy surf, placing all my pain and emotions into the sea and watching as the tide carried them away, once again I was cleansed by the salt water, as it washed over me leaving a different landscape, a new cleaner beginning.

Many times I wished June would wake when the night devil visited, mother would have to believe me, and I sobbed silently as he left the room. My body had become a carcass that was beaten and abused, the first time the night devil touched me in an adult way was the last Sharon ceased to exist, and the ugly bitch stood in her place.

⚜ Chapter Five ⚜

I trusted no one and rebuked authority of any kind feeling immense anger, afraid to voice any opinion in the home so away from the domicile deciding; I would not be used.

My schoolwork started to suffer I was fast approaching thirteen years of age and for the past two and a half years I had been abused, physically, sexually, and emotionally, I was streetwise beyond my years and feared no one from out side the home.

I was destructive towards myself and others, picking fights with my teachers giving the persona of some one who was hard, unfeeling, and not a care for any one or thing.

Our social worker visited on very few occasions, on his last visit he asked to sit in his car so we could talk, he inquire if there was anything I wanted to tell him, I looked at him then to my front door then into his eyes wondering if he would believe me, in my head I was debating the issue.

"What if you don't? I will have to go back into the house."

The tenderness I once felt returning, my vulnerability and longing to trust, I started to panic Mother would beat me again so would the night devil, there was nowhere to turn.

"No," I replied.

My harshness returning, that was the last time I saw him no one from the outside visited again; no hope of the abuse ever stopping, and I was not the only one aware of how alone and vulnerable I was, the night devil realized it too.

"See, even your social worker don't give a shit."

I knew he was right and I fantasized about killing him but realized I would never be able to summons the courage to do it; this added to my guilt. Sunday mornings was always a relaxing time,

"Get your glass of water ready" Step-father would order

"See who can catch the biggest one"

A pint glass half filled with water and each of us would go to our bedrooms and search the bedding for fleas; it was a competition that became a ritual. Step-father would kill the fleas crushing them between his thumbnails.

He would some times spray the bedding with a flit gun causing us to choke and splutter, I wished he would do it when we were not occupying the beds. When Paul asked why we had fleas mother blamed Mark, and his association with a dirty family.

"Makes me laugh, we have not had clean sheets for nearly twelve months"

Paul muttered to me, the sheets had flea shit all over them I assumed this was perfectly normal, until I asked my friend on the way to school Monday morning; how many fleas she had caught the day before, brushing it off as a joke once I realized the horror on my friends face was no act. It was then I realised that not every one had the same home life and my home was full of secrets and whispers.

The house was dirty and smelly the bedrooms were rarely cleaned, step-father had a Jackal and Hyde personality; he did the most for us in terms of recreational activities most Sundays after the contest of who can catch the biggest flea, he would take us for a long drive to the many beaches around the area. For a while we could forget and be part of a normal family, looking just like any other family unit except mother never accompanied us, rarely did the boys go with us. Mother would stay at home cooking the Sunday roast a meal I always had if I stayed with step-father, mother could not deny a meal or accuse me of being late unless she wanted to starve him and June as well. So when ever possible I would go with him and June to the beach, after the beach he went to the pub. June and I amused ourselves and on one occasion June asked if we could go and see the swans

"No I can't be bothered to walk over there"

"I will tell mum you swore last night and that you hit me" I knew mother would not hesitate to beat the hell out of me,

"Come on please its better then sitting in the car waiting for Dad to turn up pissed"

"All right but only if you promise not to throw bloody stones at the swans this time"

June agreed.

We made our way to the waste ground that used to be a tidal plain and had a few swans nesting.

"We can't be to long Dad will be leaving the pub soon, I don't want to walk home"

I was hungry and wanted dinner it had been three days since I ate, we approached the swans and the gander started to chase June, hissing wildly at her I guess he remembers her from our last visit. She ran screaming as loud as her lungs would allow flaying her arms like a possessed demon. I started to laugh I had never seen anything so funny, I was trying to follow her so she did not get lost stopping as the gander turn his attention on me

"Oh shit,"

I started to run; now it was my turn to flap my arms like a possessed fiend glancing behind me to see how much ground the gander had made, but could see it nowhere.

"June, June! Where are you"? I was screeching for her to answer and getting a little cross.

"You have had your fun come on answer me or I will leave you; right I am off"

I waited and heard a faint cry; I started to run in the direction it had come from knowing June was in trouble.

"JUNE! BLOODY ANSWER ME".

"Oh my god"

I heard a pitiful cry and scanned the area darting from cattail to cattail, hoping the gander was not waiting in this marsh land around the next bed of bogged water or plant.

"What the hell you playing at, come on we have to go"

"I can't move every time I try I sink lower and lower" she was getting very distressed and the enormity of the situation started to dawn on me

"I will go and get help can you hold on"

"No don't leave me Sharon don't go please"

"I won't go, its ok I am going to try and crawl over to you,"

Very gently I managed to reach her; June was buried up to her knees, I pulled and pulled there was a loud sucking noise,

"My shoes, I have lost my shoes"

"Forget them, they are gone,"

When we got back on hard ground we both hugged each other,

"Mothers going to kill me Sharon what about my shoes"

"She won't, maybe if it were me but you will be ok"

I was worried I would be punished for this, June's legs were filthy we looked for water to wash her.

"Pooh! June you stink, you smell like you fell in the toilet"

She never again asked to go and see the swans; my perception of them had also changed I always believed swans were serene and elegant on the lakes, and although they waddled like a duck they waddled with grace and stature how wrong was I. We made our way back to the car step-father came out of the pub he was very angry with June.

"My bloody car you silly git, you have stunk it out"

The rest of the journey was continued in silence as we pulled up outside the house; I swallowed hard and thought to my self,

"Here we go, blah, blah and more blah"

"Get your clothes off madam, where were you when this was going on"

Staring in my direction accusingly,

"She was chasing the gander away from me if Sharon had not done that I would have been bitten"

I wonder if they would be so happy if it were me probably not, one less to feed would be their attitude if I died

"Sod them"

The house was filled with the aroma of food mother was cooking the lunch music from the radio was blasting through the open windows, and every one seemed relaxed.

Sunday afternoons we were not allowed in the house come rain or shine, both parents would sleep after lunch, as soon as we had cleaned the kitchen we had to leave the house not to return until six in the evening, my brothers quite often went off on their own leaving June and I to find our own entertainment.

I would head for the local woods with June in tow we had become close, many times I had defended her against the bullies; she was spoilt by her parents and could just about get away with most things. But she never used this against me, most times sticking up for me and on a few occasions stopping mother from beating me.

Mother was waiting when June and I arrived home from school handing us a bag each we were informed new clothes had been purchased for us. I shook with excitement as I opened my bag and pulled out a brand new skirt. This was the first time I had ever had new clothes I sniffed the newness of the material and marvelled at the colour.

June threw hers on the chair and proceeded to take a drink for herself, mother ordered that she try on the garment to make sure it fitted. I raced upstairs followed by June. She pulled hers from the bag it was identical to mine, rushing back down she demanded to know why we had matching skirts. Mother explained it would stop any fighting between us, I didn't care less this was my first new skirt nothing could take away my happiness.

I was awake the following morning earlier than usual my skirt neatly laid out on the bedstead, my pleasure for all to see. Mother was already up and getting ready for her day at work, I entered the kitchen with my head held high envisioning my friend's faces as I walked into school this morning.

"Why have you got that on?"

I explained I wanted to wear it to school mother proceeded to scream at me I had put on Junes skirt, puzzled how she knew I rushed up the stairs and swapped the skirt for Junes. When I put it on I could also see they were identical in size, adding to my confusion. Making my way back down the stairs I re-entered the kitchen smiling at her.

Again she screamed at me to get the skirt off I cried with frustration explaining I had changed the skirt over.

"They are Junes skirts, you are to fat for them get it off"

I rushed up the stairs believing my whole world insane, June was perplexed with the explanation and rushed down to inform mother, she neither needed nor wanted two identical skirts. I listened intently on the stairs hoping mother would cede and allow me to keep one. I was ordered to leave my new skirt on mothers bed, it disappeared as fast as it came, leaving me bewildered.

We awoke one morning to a sound not often heard

"What's that?" Mark asked sarcastically.

It was step-father singing and that means one thing as far as we were concerned, no beatings.

"Why are you so happy?"

"Have you won the pools?" June asked, my brothers and I were on the stairs listening attentively,

"Cheeky! I am always happy, I have a new car you should see it your mother bought it for me" he beamed.

"Pity she did not spend the money on shoes for us" Paul remarked.

"I think these plastic shoes are bloody great especially when they get to small and mother cuts the backs off and makes us wear them for another six months as backless sandals, that just about pisses off all the kids around here because they all want a pair" I added bitterly.

Both the boys started to laugh and returned upstairs, I went into the kitchen to join June.

"Come on you two get ready, I will take you for a ride in my new car"

"Will you wear your bus driver's hat dad?"

"Yes I have it here come on"

June and I got into the car excited about the journey ahead, and the response and stares we got when step-father drove with a bus mans hat he had found at work.

People thought he was a chauffer we girls laughed and giggled, it seemed weird to me how some of my friends envied me.

"You are so lucky Sharon your dad takes you out makes cycles for you my dad just drinks" Caroline commented, sounding jealous.

Oh! How I wished I could share my true feelings with Caroline. A closed door can hold many a dark secret, and many people hid behind a closed mind,

When we returned step-father went back out leaving us at home, June disappeared to her friends house Paul and Mark had already left the house before our return.

I was on my own looking in the fridge to see what I could eat; I took a nibble from every thing and a raw sausage I ate with gusto, and then left the house bumping into Bobby- Joe.

"I am so bored I will be glad to get back to school tomorrow" she moaned

"Me to I don't know why school's are used for voting, where you off to?"

"No where in particular just roaming around no one home at my house"

Bobby-Joe thought for a while

"I know, how about we go down the woods"

We staying for a few hours returning later in the afternoon, walking towards my house I noticed step-fathers car and knew he would be drunk.

"Your dad's home shall we go in your house?"

"Um no, I um, I need to talk to Sylvia you coming?"

We were going into Sylvia's gate when step-father appeared in the street

"I need you to go to the shop!" he ordered.

"Get two tins of beans."

He was very drunk dropping his coins on the floor and was staggering when he tried to pick them up.

"Will you come with me?" I almost pleaded.

"No; I don't fancy walking all the way down to the shops but I will wait here for you, we can go to Sylvia's after"

I was annoyed with myself for not getting out of the street sooner I kept repeating to myself

"Beans, Beans!"

Afraid I would forget what was needed getting it wrong would be signing my own death warrant and the beans word ran around head.

Getting the peas and running all the way home proud I had made up for the lost time talking to a friend.

"Got them wont be a minute I will just take then inside"

"Ok, hang on I will come with you"

I was glad Bobby-Joe was coming with me and leaving my friend at the back door I handed the peas to him.

"How the fucking hell can we have peas on toast?" he bellowed.

Edging my way towards the back door I promised to go straight away and exchange them, lifting a tin over his head he threw it at me knocking me off my feet in a heap next to the back door. I needed to get up looking to see where Bobby-Joe was, not wanting the embarrassment of my friend watching the beating. She had ran the minute he started to shout I was thankful for this

"Please dad, please!"

Grabbing for my hair he lifted me up ripping it out by the roots;

continuing to swing me around like a rag doll his fist connected with my face, banging my skull against the wall I could see flashes of light with each thud to my head, my body started to go numb.

It seemed to go on forever, things started to slow down step-father was sounding as though he was under water.

"Just let me die," I no longer cared, when he had exhausted himself he calmly walked into the lounge leaving me on the kitchen floor; returning and screaming,

"Money was short I am feeding some one else's bastard," he lashed out again kicking me sharply in the hip walking back into the lounge and returning before the door had time to close.

"You are your father's bastard he didn't want you he won't ever acknowledge you as his daughter, you are mine to do as I please, bitch"

Kicking me harder this time catching me on the side of the head I knew I had to get up off the floor, before he returned; he seemed almost robotic in his movements I believed he was completely insane and I was going to die.

"Why am I supposed to feed and look after his slag of a daughter?"

Stamping on my right ankle I felt the bone snap, the pain seared through me, talking in an agitated state walking up and down the kitchen kicking me every time he passed talking incoherently. I cowered in the corner watching his feet and looking for a sign of him lifting them off the floor. Step-father stopped by the sink and gazed out of the window, all had gone quiet his ravings had stopped and a strange stillness had fallen.

"Why do you like me to hurt you?" he asked without turning to face me

Terrified, I did not know how to answer for fear of provoking him further, no words could I find no sound to my voice, just sheer terror was all I could feel.

"Go and wash yourself," he very calmly said without looking at me.

There was blood splattered everywhere I had not been aware of the blood, washing my face I could see the damage that had been caused, it was only then I cried wanting to scream pushing the towel into my mouth to muffle the sound, I sank to the floor weeping, my shoe was tight on my ankle and the pain shooting up my right leg, making it feel heavy.

Step-father shouted for me to get out of the bathroom I thought about locking myself in, but knew he could easily knock the door down besides; I was very weak and did not have the fight in me to be bothered. He looked at me and said I made him do it my face was feeling tight; my eyes closing from the swelling and my body hurt all over.

"I'm sorry,"

I was trying to say, but my words stuck in the pit of stomach, my head was going to explode my vision blurred I was swaying; desperately trying to stand my right ankle felt heavy and the pain making me physically sick, trying frantically not to show he had hurt me my knees buckled.

Step-father lifted me onto the settee and started to attend my cuts, all the time reiterating I was to blame. I no longer cared if he killed me, and it would be a relief.

That night my ankle was hurting bad and I found it hard to sleep, the covers felt heavy upon my leg but I was afraid to say anything. I was angry with mother when seeing my injuries asked what I had done this time to deserve it.

Getting ready for school step-father reminded me.

"Don't forget you fell down the stairs and landed on the door frame"

In a strange way I felt I was doing some thing good when I lied about my injuries, protecting them I believed they may start to like me a little.

"We don't want everyone knowing what an idiot you are, do we?"

It was hard for me to walk but I did not want to stay home from school this would mean having to be there when step-father returned from the pub, but the pain became severe I had to get medical help I knew I was hurt bad, the afternoon's playtime I pretended to fall letting every one believe my injury were sustained at school, they phoned for an ambulance,

"Oh my!" my teacher joked,

"What a clumsy person you are first you fall down the stairs at home and then in the playground, People are going to think someone else is inflicting your injuries."

If only he could see the pictures in my head I smiled politely my parents were informed and step-father came to the hospital to pick me up.

"What have you told them?" stooping over me menacingly

"Nothing, I told them I did it in the playground,"

"Well I didn't do this to you so don't you even think to lie," he was gripping my arm as he spoke, the unsaid words, I knew what he meant.

"I know you did not I fell in the playground,"

My ankle was broke and set in a caste and I was to return in two days, the trip home was agonizing every bump in the road made me cry out.

"You can be so clumsy, cant you?"

The tone in step-fathers voice gentle and caring, it was a side I had not observed before, on arriving home he parked the car on the pavement and gently lifted me carrying me towards the back door, mother appeared brandishing a stick.

"Where the hell have you been you little bastard?"

I tried to protect my foot with my hand step-father pushed mother away from me, I was stunned no one had ever defended me before; gently he placed me on the sofa.

I liked this sort of attention but the look mother gave I was going to pay dearly for it, this was the closest I had ever felt towards him.

"You boys will to do her paper round," he ordered.

The following morning mother was frowning menacingly oh how I was going to suffer for this attention.

Academically, all three of us were above average and good at sport; we represented our school and achieved reputations as forces to be reckoned with. Accomplishing my bronze in the Duke of Edinburgh's award scheme; I was proud of this attainment only three others managed it how I hoped mother would feel the same. It was my willingness to please that drove me on; I needed her to believe what step-father was doing and wanted her love desperately.

I was captain of the netball team and always top of my class in the term exams, but my attitude towards my teachers marred all my good attainments, making me stand out as an outlandish trouble maker who could not be controlled. I had built a wall around me protecting my emotional vulnerability; no one was going to destroy it.

"You will have to stay home for a few weeks while your leg heals"

"I will be ok I don't mind school and I have some crutches the hospital gave"

"No you have to stay here! Oh by the way the school is taking the whole of the net ball team away as a thank you for winning most games last term"

"Brilliant, when"

"Next week so I believe"

"Oh I should be ok I have my crutches"

"You can't go you have to stay here if you can't go to school then you can't go out at all" mother sneered.

"Please I will go to school I want to go to school"

I hated staying at home school term was the happiest time for me; it gave me respite from the traumas of home, and a guaranteed meal.

"You are not bloody going; I don't want to hear any more about it"

I hobbled away to cry, how I wished I were going with them no friends were allowed to visit, I had no contact with the outside world, the weeks past slowly step-father being attentive in a good way waking to another morning; I had got into a routine of housework.

Today I am having the cast changed I excitedly told Mark, step-father was taking me before lunch I was thrilled to be going back to school, although the six weeks I had been home was probably the calmest it had ever been.

"When can I return to school?" I asked the doctor

"My! This has to be a first; some one actually wants to go to school"

Teasing, ruffling my hair I wondered why doctors always had to dishevel people's hair.

"There's no reason why you can not return tomorrow we are going to fit you with another cast and a boot which allows you to put pressure on the foot. Are you sure you want to go to school some kids can be pretty spiteful."

"Thanks; I don't mind if they do I just need to go back"

"You may find walking a little difficult; and mastering the stairs to start but persevere, it will become easier."

"Oh I have already mastered the stairs and walked on it from the time I broke it, every day I have done all the cleaning in the house mother did not want me to become idle"

I arrogantly replied looking to step-father as I spoke.

"You have been doing all this since you broke it?"

The doctor replied shocked, looking to step-father for an explanation, he coughed nervously,

"Oh Sharon stop exaggerating she has made her bed the last few days, that's all"

The colour in his cheeks rising to a healthy glow,

Yeah right on, lying dick, I was thinking to my self as I smiled sweetly at him realizing I had him squirming and it felt bloody good, I was on a roll.

"Yes I need to go back to school as soon as possible the house is a danger to live in"

"Danger"

The doctor inquired whilst holding my hand waiting for some thing unpleasant to be said, step-father fiddled awkwardly with his jacket,

"Sharon its time to go, move it"

Clenching his teeth in a threatening manner,

"Hold on a minute,"

The doctor turned to step-father who had positioned himself behind him glaring at me he knew exactly what I meant.

"I mean I broke my leg didn't I? Well the house has steps, stairs to go to bed, steps everywhere that's all; why? What did you think I meant"?

"Oh I see you are a strange one"

I smiled looking to the night devil his face relaxed I thought to myself yep, you have the same images in your head as me, you are a bully and a bastard oh, and you also have a small dick. I continued to smile at him the nurse interrupted my thoughts.

"Bye Sharon we will see you in clinic in another week keep up the good work"

We got into the car for the journey home I knew I would have to pay for being smug.

"I will drop you home then I am off to the pub do you need anything before I go?" he was still being pleasant; this was puzzling I was waiting for the ear bashing from my recent show.

"Um, no I can't think of any thing,"

I took great pleasure in informing mother I was going back to school the following day,

"About bloody time your ass is getting wider with all the sitting around.

The following morning I was up and dressed early

"Don't forget to clean the stairs and brush the floor in the lounge before you go to school. Oh! Don't forget to peel the spuds for tea tonight"

Mother ordered.

"How can I do that? I can't stand without my crutches and I won't be able to get on my hands and knees to brush the floor with this boot on?"

"The doc says you are ok for school you lazy bitch, then you are ok to do some fucking work and don't forget after school your paper round, your brothers have done enough for you"

Slamming the back door as she left giving me no time to answer, and getting on my knees to brush the floor step-father came into the room

"What are you doing?"

"Cleaning, mother said,"

He cut me short,

"Bugger your mother give it to me I will do it"

This was new step-father sticking up for me again with out making any demands either, the walk to school took me longer than I thought, but I was happy to be back.

"Sharon what the hells that on your foot"

Bobby-Joe was laughing my other friends joined in, I told them to keep their voices down every one will want one, I joked.

"How did the trip go?" I asked feeling rather envious of them.

"What trip?" Jeannette answered

"The trip the school paid for because we are so bloody good at netball"

"There was no trip; well not one I have been invited"

"I don't understand, perhaps"

It suddenly dawned on me mother had lied

"What a bitch Jesus Christ, what a bitch"

I began to understand that mother liked to play mind games; the day went well I had arranged to go to the fair on Sunday with my friends knowing I need not ask permission, Sunday afternoon was my time to do as I pleased. The walk home from school was magical I was with all my friends as we talked and mucked around.

"Sharon what happened the day you went to the shops?"

"Nothing happened why you want to know"

"I saw how angry he was; I thought he had murdered you, fucking hell girl his face looked like a bulldogs chewing on a wasp."

"I was in school the following day that's when I broke my leg, my dads not too bad"

"Your mother told us all to stay away; she said you were not well I feel stupid now" Bobby-Joe laughed.

No one knew what was really going on in the home the lack of food the beatings; we had become good at covering up the unsavoury activities, ashamed of what others would think humiliated what I was allowing, my house was full of whispers and secrets.

I asked Mark how to get the money for the rides

"Go underneath the rides and look around the ground People lose their change when they sit on the rides we have found loads"

"Really, I wouldn't have thought about that"

Sunday morning I asked for some money from my earnings on the paper round knowing the answer before hand. Approaching the fair several of my friends were waiting

"How you going to walk in the mud with that shoe and boot, you will slip and slide every where?" Jenny commented sarcastically.

"Not your problem is it? So just leave it out, ok?"

Jenny and I were not the closest of friends there was a little rivalry between us. I was captain of the netball team, something Jenny had tried hard to achieve, we were both competent swimmers I only just managing to keep ahead of her. Jenny was referring to my shoe which was made of the cheapest plastic.

"Come on you two let's have a day of peace no school no teachers, and no bloody parents"

Bobby-Joe coaxed as she started to run towards the big wheel.

I walked behind fed up looking the odd one out my friends never said any thing about the condition of my clothes, but I knew I stood out as a little different; they had all the latest fashions the best coats and the best shoes. I had second hand clothes from a younger sister but had not really noticed it before, and was not really bothered about clothes and fashion. Recently though, I had started to notice and so were others and wearing this boot for my injured leg made me stand out more.

Many children were teased because of the poor way they were dressed but not I, nor my brothers I had never lost a confrontation not even with the boys.

My attitude was, if you beat me to the ground and can't keep me there then you better run, this attitude probably had a lot to do with why I was never picked on.

"Come on slow coach, are you ok Sharon what's wrong?"

"Its nothing its going to take me a little longer to walk with this stupid boot, I have to go to the toilet I will meet you all here in a minute"

"Go on then we will meet in a minute, are you sure about the big wheel"

"Quite sure Bobby-Joe honest, I won't be long"

"We are all going on the big wheel you coming or not, it's the last time we will ask"

"I said No what part of no don't you understand Jeannette"

"Ok calm down, go, who the hell cares"

Jeannette knew she was pressing all the right buttons winding me up a treat; making my way towards the toilets looking behind until my friends were out of sight, I could hit Jeannette so hard I fumed to myself.

Out of sight of my friends I made my way beneath the Waltzers, it was a little scary a penny shone through the dirt and looking up I could see the ride above through the gapes in the floor. I heard a roaring noise and the whole structure started to shake violently as the engine started up. I scurried quickly to get out not sure what to expect as the ride built up momentum, the floor above started to rock, the noise deafening. Taking this opportunity to have a better look around using the sound of the ride to cover any noise I make, easy pickings lucky to find nearly one pound I had never had this much money before, the ride was stopping, I stayed underneath until it started again and then left, it was easy to blend back into the crowds but being underneath the ride had also made me realize that food and money were plentiful, as I eyed up the un-eaten hot-dogs in the surrounding bins.

"Where have you been we thought you may have gone home"

"I went to the toilet there was a long queue, I told you I was going"

"Ok strops, slow down" Jeannette remarked

I started to tire of Jeanette's attitude; I was not prepared to have my whole day ruined by her mindless twaddle, I felt embarrassed about my scavenging and the tell tale smell of food on my breath. When the time is right I will have a word in her ear.

"Come on let's go in the haunted house,"

Bobby-Joe suggested, we joined the queue and chatted away about school and what they should expect in the haunted house, teasing each other and guessing who was going to be the most scared.

"When are you having that awe full boot off, we need you for the netball team"

"Next week hopefully, the doctor says I have healed really well"

Entering the haunted house most of the girls screamed and hung onto each other before we got near the activities, I couldn't understand why it was suppose to be frightening. But I was enjoying my time with friends, even Jeannette seemed to calm down a little.

I was able to buy a hot dog and go on the fruit machines,

"I wish today would never end" enjoying the last ride on the merry go-round, glancing over towards my friends studying their faces wondering what really went on in their homes. Three days later I was free from my boot and able to return to the sports I loved, the summer holidays were once again upon us, the last day of term all my friends were excited, with a heavy heart I walked home six weeks of boredom and no food, survival of the fittest is what the holidays meant to me.

I was starting to attract the attentions of the young men especially some of my brother's friends who were looking at me as a young woman, rather than the younger sister. Step-father was quick to stop this attention chasing off any who made the slightest comment or showed the smallest amount of interest. I how ever, did not look at boys in any other way than friends.

One good male friend was Kenny who was fourteen years of age, a few months older than I he had a brother the same age as June named Keith. Often we would meet and hang out together a purely platonic relationship; June had a small tent that was pitched in the back garden. The sun shone bright and boredom had reached all of us, we were laying on our stomachs talking in the tent with our feet out of the door, we were quite comfortable in our canvas den.

"Shall we go to the fair then?" Keith suggested.

We were trying to decide where to go later in the afternoon; I never tired of the fair and the magical feel at night when it was brightly lit.

"I don't have any money but I will come along and watch all of you"

"I will ask dad for some money Sharon and then we can share"

"Thanks June; lets just wait, maybe I will get some money from him."

"I will get you some money I will nick it off me old dear"

Kenny meant it; he would steal what ever he needed from his mother and her many boyfriends. He would also swear at them, run wild in the street and stay out all night, if he pleased. Very much the same as most children living in the surrounding area; I envied their lack of fear, glancing at my watch; we had to keep an eye on the time step-father would be back from the pub and I wanted to make sure no one was in the garden on his return.

We settled back down and talked about our dreams and aspirations, Keith wanted to be a train robber Kenny, was going to move to London and become a gangster June, a nurse, I had no idea, I was only able to concentrate on the day at hand, my thoughts never led into the future we laughed at quirky jokes and teased each other about family. Suddenly Keith and Kenny were pulled from the tent, June lifted the side to see what had grappled them, and horrified to see step-father, he had come home early and seeing four pairs of legs protruding out of the tent he yanked the two he did not recognize.

Keith and Kenny stood up as June and I scurried out of the tent and to our feet in record time.

"Home you two little bastards go on, fuck off, gets out of here"

"Mr Arscott can I ask you some thing?"

I was stunned by Kenny and intrigued what he wanted to ask.

"I am not Mr Arscott lad, now piss off home and don't let me catch you in here again"

Kenny was taken aback by step-fathers denial.

"You are Sharon's dad?"

I started to shake a little Kenny was always a cheeky sod and not easily frightened, his long hair matted by the lack of washing his fringe dangling in his eyes and grass stains on his shirtsleeves, and the knees to his trousers threadbare he fitted well into the area we lived.

"Piss off home you little git"

"When I am grown I am going to marry Sharon, MR ARSCOTT"

Kenny smirked emphasizing the Mr.

"When you are grown fuck face! You little pip squeak Piss off, get out,"

"Dad, what are you doing? Stop it, they are our friends"

June was getting angry at the treatment her father was dishing out to our friends; Keith had already left the garden he was younger and not so brave some might even say not so stupid.

"Kenny, please go, please! We can meet later"

I interrupted holding his arm and willing him in the direction of his own home.

"Get here you fucking bitch what you doing let him go"

"Leave her alone you fucking dog" Kenny shouted in my defence, step-father's aggressive attitude towards them and now me, were agitating Kenny.

"Who the hell you talking to you little shit"

Step-father grabbed my arm and dragged me behind him I was trying to usher Kenny away with eye contact.

"WHATS YOU'RE PROBLEM, OLD MAN?"

Step-father lunged at him June and I started to scream Kenny managed to side step him, and then stayed at a safe distance.

"You little yellow assed idiot, gobbing off like that, don't let me catch you here ever again"

Step-father was fuming I thought he would have a heart attack, I was going to get the full brunt of his anger; Kenny was dancing around swearing and jeering him I had never seen any one stand up to him in this manner, secretly enjoying his humiliation he could not strike out at Kenny as he would I, or so I believed.

Suddenly, with out warning step-father grabbed Kenny punching him on the arm, Kenny retaliated by kicking him in the leg and calling him an asshole, Kenny ran heading towards his own house over taking Keith who had been sitting on the pavement, step-father was in hot pursuit Keith desperately tried to out run him and was crying as he closed in. He ran past Keith, it was Kenny he wanted, June and I laughed as Keith sat back on the pavement breathing hard; he was barley able to speak his fear obvious.

"BLOODY HELL what's your old mans problem he's a frigging lunatic"

"Your brother started it he should have just left and he's the frigging lunatic not my dad"

I decided not to comment either way secretly agreeing with Keith, as we spoke step-father came back into the street

"Dad this idiot has just said you're a frigging lunatic" pointing to Keith, with an accusing finger.

"Oh for Christ sake June, you stupid bitch now he's going to kill me"

Keith panicked dragging himself to a standing position and started to run crying out aloud, he ran in the opposite direction.

"Get in doors both of you" step-father was breathing very heavy I walked behind him praying he would drop dead from a heart attack, fearing my punishment

"Jesus the little shit couldn't half move don't let the little bastard back in here if I catch him I will kill him"

Warning both of us about the dangers of letting boys into the house when alone, I looked to him and knew his reasons for reacting as he did were very different from the explanation he gave.

"They are friend's dad calm down you should not have dragged them out of the tent"

I wished I could have the same freedom of speech I would have said a lot more.

"Is that what you think Sharon?"

"No dad I think he disrespected you he was in the wrong"

What I really wanted to say was,

"Piss off you pervert, glad you have met some one who is not afraid"

I was surprised how step-father had dealt with the situation and sure the after math of such a confrontation would result in me being severely beaten, but he just went on and on about what boys do, and don't want.

"Can we go to the fair dad?"

"Ok but no hanging around the dodgems like the others and home by 6 o'clock, no later"

He gave us a sixpence each we left the house happy and excited by the coming event, walking towards the large grassland where the fair had been erected we could see Kenny and Keith.

"Don't talk to them they are asshole look what they did to dad"

"I know they are June but they are our friends come on what dad don't know he won't grieve over"

"Bloody hell Sharon your dad"

I shot a stare at Kenny, explaining June was a little upset and I think he should apologies what was said about her dad

"Sorry June"

Keith said lowering his head.

"Not you Keith, I mean Kenny, and maybe if you apologize to dad he will let you back into the garden"

"I am not apologizing to that asshole I have no death wish I am staying well away"

"Christ Kenny apologies to June, come on I want to enjoy the rest of the day in peace"

I demanded he apologized to her but when June and Keith went on the big wheel I had time to ask what had happened when step-father chased him.

"I know he's your dad Sharon but the mans a complete fucking idiot he chased me all the way to my house, when I reached me gate I thought thank god I am safe, I looked up and the fat bastard was still coming at me, I ran into the house and looked out of the window he was stood at the gate swearing at me. So I gave him the V sign, the fucking asshole ran into me house chased me up the stairs. I had to jump from me fucking bedroom window, wish me old lady had been home she would have kicked his ass straight out of there."

I was laughing so hard I had to sit on the ground his rendition of the experience was colourful indeed

"He's not my dad his surname is Davie the same as Junes, she's my half sister"

"Tell him to piss off he can't talk to you like that my old ladies boyfriends would not dare talk to us like it"

How I wished I could tell him more but I did not trust him enough,

"He's not that bad Kenny, you just caught him on an off day" I lied.

"One other thing Kenny, I will not marry you either fancy telling him that you idiot"

"One day Sharon Arscott, I will marry you" he replied adamantly.

The rest of the day went well and as we returned home I was starting to realize that step-father had weaknesses.

On the way home June, decided to visit a friend I walked into the house unaware my brother was being beaten upstairs, I heard the shouting and blows from the belt as it connected to the intended target I wanting to run, but fear was overcome with a need to know how badly my brother was hurt. Hearing his pleas for mercy I knew in my heart he must be badly wounded.

Tiptoeing up the stairs everything went quiet barely audible sobs from Paul was all I could hear. He sounded weak I knew that feeling all to well deciding to go back outside and wait until step-father passed out on the sofa. Turning to descend the stairs the step behind me creaked I smelled the familiar stench of stale alcohol, I wanted to disappear I turned and was looking into the face of my nightmares. The feral look in his eyes told me I was in deep trouble, lunging at me I lost all bodily function hoping he was too angry to notice the puddle forming on the floor.

"You dirty fucking bitch,"

he screamed in my face I was paralyzed with fear as blow after blow to my body had me unable to breath, pulling me around like a rag doll by the hair I could hear the roots being ripped out as I concentrated on staying on my feet, knowing if I fell he would kick me repeatedly, and I did not want to have to go through another broken bone. I lost my footing and tumbled down the stairs he jumped on me as I crashed into the wall in the passage below, the hair was ripped from my skull, he was tossing me around like a whale does a seal just before the kill. He was eighteen stone and six feet plus the muscles in his arm were wider than my waist.

It seemed to go on forever the only thought going through my mind was hoping he would miss me on the next punch. When he had finished he stormed into the lounge cursing and swearing. I looked to the front door

"Freedom, so close Jesus Christ he's a bloody lunatic I hate him one day when I am old enough I am going to leave"

Again fantasizing about beating him

"One day he will hit me and I will kick his ass."

I noticed the splats of blood on my clothes looking around the tiny passage I started to giggle I tried to stop, looking around the floor I noticed an ant scurrying between the skirting boards. One two, three, a whole colony of them Oh how I wished I were small become so insignificant invisible. I tried to climb the stairs needing to have a rest, and also to check my brother. The stairs seemed to have got steeper afraid to make any noise this would provoke him further; I had managed to climb eight steps when he re-appeared at the foot of them.

"You still here?" he screamed

"Get your ugly face in your room you thieving lying stinking bastard."

"Yes dad! Yes dad!"

I replied wanting to see where he was he started at me again I tried desperately to get away but had no strength.

"Please dad I am sorry,"

"You will be,"

he snarled back I tripped on the last step, step-father started to drag me towards my bedroom I thought this time I would die, I could take no more and just wanted to stop breathing just let it all go. Step-father threw me into my room and staggered back down the stairs.

"Stay there you two bastards till your mother gets home. I'll teach you to steal from me."

I heard him go all the way down the stair and the lounge door slam, I started to sob quietly and was relieved he would not attack me sexually Paul was in the house. He never did this when others were around during the day, but knew nothing would stop him beating me to death. I was aware there was no one who cared for either of us, our own father had abandoned us and so had our grandparents. Waiting for what seemed forever I knew eventually he would fall asleep in a drunken haze; this was the normal turn of events. I needed to see Paul he needed help but fear of step-father catching me, far outweighed any thoughts of helping Paul, I heard some one quietly climbing the stairs.

"Oh! My God, he's coming back!"

I scanned the room looking for somewhere to hide two beds were all that was in the room looking at the window I thought about jumping out of it, but what if he catches me? He would definitely kill me besides; I would have to come home eventually. I had given up all hope and exhausted all solutions for my escape; I held Molly Dolly close and waited my fate, Mark appeared at the door. I truly believed I would have a heart attack through sheer terror.

"What's happened what have you both done?"

"I don't know what it's about he just went crazy Paul is dead,"

I felt an urge to laugh again

"We have to get out of here, where's Dad?"

Mark explained he had passed out on the sofa and that we needed to get Paul and leave the house Mark was in a panic as we entered the boy's bedroom Paul was laying face down.

"Are you OK?"

Paul had pretended to be knocked out he heard the beating I took and believed he would be back for him.

"You have to walk we need to get out before he wakes, we'll meet Mother and she will do something"

Paul was bleeding I started to cry the blood had soaked through his t-shirt.

"Look at your face Sharon you look like a monster."

"Well at least I don't look like this normally."

We started to laugh and take fun out of each others injuries getting hysterical, Mark helped Paul to his feet.

I held Paul's other arm and slowly Mark and I helped him to the landing. I asked if he comes back what do we do,

"Run Sharon run like hell because he will kill us if he wakes."

Again I started to giggle the blood pumping through my veins I really did not want to have to deal with this.

"Stop giggling it's not funny," Mark could not understand how we found this situation funny, I did not, I was bloody terrified of going down the stairs but I could not stop giggling.

We started the long slow descent of the stairs it was a tight squeeze for all three to go together but none of us offered to be last. I noticed where I had peed was almost dry but had stained the course carpet that was layed in the middle of each step. I wanted to run it was taking to long the creaking of the stairs amplified by the stillness of the house. We banged into the wall, manoeuvring the bend was a work of art, reaching the bottom I noticed a handful of my hair moving idly in the draft from the ill fitting front door, blood stains on the walls flashed me back to the fear I felt not an hour before.

"We have to go out the front door we can't go through the living room he will wake."

Paul was trembling, his legs unable to hold him up.

"Come on," Mark urged him,

"It's just a little way."

I grasped the door lock and slowly turned the knob freedom was just behind this wooded door, then it happened, behind us the lounge door squeaked the familiar sound we all knew when the door was opened, we hung onto each other with bated breath waiting to see who was to be attacked first. I closed my eyes and prayed for the lord to take me first after what seemed for ever I had to look behind me, the draft had caused the door to open slightly on its own. Paul told us to leave him and get ourselves out he could not make it any further.

"No!" Mark cried,

"We all stay together Come on! You can do it it's not far"

I was not sure about staying together if step-father appeared; my ass was out of there I felt no loyalty at this time each to their own. Cautiously I opened the front door it started to creak, looking behind towards the lounge door waiting once more with bated breath, I flung open the door and we stepped onto the front garden.

"Come on! Let's run!"

"We can't we have to help Paul Come on! We need to go and meet Mother."

Mark was sure mother would do some thing I just wanted to run, run as fast as my legs would carry me. Eventually getting to the bus stop we had an hour's wait hiding in the bushes until the bus arrived.

"Look what Dad has done to these two"

Mark spat at mother.

"What did you two do to make your father angry?"

"He thinks we stole sixpence off him but honest mum I did not"

Paul was hardly audible as he tried to protest his innocence I looked to her with revulsion in my heart, knowing she would do nothing to make sure it never happened again.

"I took sixpence this morning I needed it for change for my bus fare, you three wait outside and I will calm him down."

It was never mentioned again nor was there any medical assistance for Paul and my injuries.

Sixteen years of age Paul still trying to please our parents joined the navy believing they would be proud of him; he never returned to the home and left the navy after only a year settling in Scotland. Before he left Devon for good he asked mother to sign as guarantor for a three thousand-pound loan after receiving the check he left with no intentions of ever repaying it.

"One way or another they will pay me for all the money they have stolen off me and for all the beatings they gave"

I wished I could do the same only my abuse was getting worse how I envied Paul leaving.

I missed my brother very much the closeness we once had in the children's home was gone we had learned through experience to look after ourselves. Mark was now the one to take the physical beatings from step-father; mother did not seem to care choosing to ignore the bruises. Mark and I remained close in some ways we looked to each other for guidance

"Sports day today Sharon are you in many races?"

"Yes, long jump and javelin and relay"

I proudly pronounced

"Are you coming to watch?" Mark inquired of mother.

"I don't have time to sit around watching kids running around a field"

Was the sarcastic comment given back to his query.

No one came to spur us along just our selves I sat on the grass bank watching the others; I had won all my races finishing first was expected of me by my teachers.

The key to the front door was on a string hanging on my neck, we belonged to the group known as latchkey kids, I was swirling it around while engrossed in the events unfolding before me, taking in the scene the clouds Fluffy flying high, the sky blue and peaceful, feelings enveloped me as I remembered happy times; I smiled going over in my mind the attic in the boys home life was simple we were free from pain and innocent of cruelty. The voices around me started to fade the heat from the sun enveloping like a shawl. I imagined the heat as angel's wings surrounding me with love and keeping me safe, some times I felt so sad I believed my heart would shatter into a thousand tiny pieces, loneliness was a friend I knew well the deep abyss of fear my companion I wanted to share with many my thoughts and experiences I wanted mother to love me, and step-father to protect me.

"Come on we have to get home before he does"

The school was allowing the children to leave early

I noticed my finger no longer held the key, panic took hold

"What's wrong?"

I HAVE LOST THE KEY"

Hysterically I was trying to explain

"Don't move from the spot I will get a stone and you can throw it maybe it will land in the same spot"

I threw it whilst simulating swivelling the string, after the third attempt Mark started to get angry with me.

"I am not coming home with you I have nothing to do with this you were given the fucking key not me"

Again he chased the stone as it landed on the grass

"Please make it right I will do any thing if you let us find it" I was praying as I had never prayed before.

"I've got it yes! Yes! Bloody hell look its here"

I stood up still not quite believing our luck; we grabbed each other and started to dance hugging and screaming shouting and singing.

"Let's go, run lets get home and out again before he gets home I want to finish my paper round early"

Mark knew he had only one year left in this god forsaken life, he too joined the armed forces it was his ticket out he also never returned to the family home.

⊰ Chapter Six ⊱

I LIVE IN A HOUSE WITH THREE OTHER PEOPLE BUT was very much alone and isolated step-father was still abusing me, mother more mentally and verbally, although at times physical. I would try very hard not to do or say anything to set them off but without my brothers I was very much a target for their frustrations. Step-father had also started to attack me more frequently in the daylight hours pinning me to the floor as I begged and pleading for him to stop, after he had finished he would roll off me telling me what a tease I was letting me know the next time he would go further, I would straighten my clothing and make my way to the bathroom, some times being physically sick after he tried to force me to perform oral sex. He never succeeded but the beatings were getting harder the torture more vile, how I dare rebuke his advances. I scrubbed my body till it bled trying to get rid of the feeling of his hands and the putrid smell of his odours, but I could never wash him off. Going over and over what had I done this time to provoke him. Yearning for my real father to rescue me hoping some one would catch him this was my only hope, step-father had made every one in the house believe I was a liar, I would wait in the bathroom for a while the alcohol takes its toll. I was able to get back outside to the safety of the streets If only the walls in this house could speak, I believe if people could see what went on in this space they would be horrified, abuse to many is a word with guessed images to me and sadly many others it's a living breathing emotion filled with metaphors that will always be, I had made my own Pandora's box and filed away many disgusting and disturbing experiences. One day my box will be opened and the contents spilled onto the floor.

If only I could find the strength to fight back at night but I never did and woke to find him by my bed many times, lifting my spirit from the dead carcass he ravished watching from a higher place where only I knew the way escaping to my dreams, imaginings I could continue from one night to another. Finding solace I had been born free to dream.

Summer holidays were worst when my brothers left the home, remembering our adventures together and when hungry we would pick apples from nearby orchards or blackberries, although the blackberries also had maggots and we would have to be treated for the infestation, but a price all were willing to pay. Hunger also had its price when trying to find food we came across a clay pit and got into making different things, a nice square bowel, plates, any thing was possible in our make believe world, June also joined in.

"Where have you been" mother demanded to know.

"Making things, we have had a great time" June enthused

"Start stripping off you little bastards, tomorrow Paul and Mark will wear a dress Sharon, you will wear your brother's clothes"

We stripped as ordered mother started to pull at my hair "come on faster bitch"

Instinctively I knew I was going to be her whipping boy, trying to hasten my pace a searing pain ran down my back, mother lifted the belt again over her head smashing it down on my right arm.

"Bitch don't you dare fucking talk to me this way?"

"SORRY Mum, PLEASE I WILL BE GOOD"

Although I was not sure what I had said the other three left the kitchen afraid they were next.

"Stand still or I will stab you"

This kind of talk terrified me mother produced a scrubbing brush that was used for the floor,

"Here start cleaning"

Getting on my knees I proceeded to scrub the floor believing she had gone totally insane.

"What the fucking hell you doing, you taking the piss"

"Washing the floor like you said" I answered in a subdued tone.

"Not the floor you stupid bitch wash yourself start scrubbing"

Delicately, I rubbed my arms.

"Are you deliberately being dumb? Harder bitch harder" forcing the brush into my skin it felt as though my flesh was being ripped from my bones,

"Took more effort than that to get dirty... OK GIVE IT TO ME, I am going to show you how to wash yourself"

Spraying spittle in my face as she screamed her venomous threats, starting at my neck and making her way down my back my hair tangled in the course bristles I believed I would faint with the pain

"There nice and pink, over in the corner and dry off stand with your arms in the air"

"Can I have a towel?"

Mother started to laugh sarcastically

"You want a towel? Piss off I have enough washing to do with out a towel stand in the corner and drip dry"

I stood as told listening how gentle mother was with June; I hate that bitch, I thought to my self willing mother to drop dead. Fuck off ass hole, bastard, bitch, dickhead I thought to myself, trying to remember every nasty word.

"Face the wall you ugly bitch I don't want your ugly mug watching me and remember I can read your thoughts"

I did as told hoping mother would allow me to soon dress; I did not want any one coming to the house and seeing me naked. Although no one would have, mother would cover up the abuse that was going on in the home.

"Jesus Christ lard ass how the hell did you get such a fat ass look at that ass kids it's just as ugly as her face, it sticks out as far as your ears"

My arms became heavy and I wanted to drop them to the sides gingerly I lowered them very slightly, this gave a little relief but the heaviness soon returned.

"Please hurry up"

I thought to myself counting the bricks which had been painted the dirtiest blue I had ever seen, to distract me from my pain. Each time some one passed by I cringed, If I dropped my arms I would pay severely for my lack of disobedience, listening to the others getting dressed I envied their existence, I wanted to turn my head and look behind but frightened mother was watching, waiting for me to disobey. She would be justified to attack and I was not going to do anything to aggravate the situation.

I sensed some one behind me and felt their stares on my naked back, mother whispered in my ear,

"Go and dress you ugly cow I have seen enough of your bulging ass you need to fucking diet, you are getting to fat."

I hesitated unsure to move, was she doing what she had in the past, talk in a whispered tone and then deny any knowledge of the conversation between us, she had done this before making me look a liar giving mother justification to beat me.

"For Christ's sake get your ugly ass out of the kitchen NOW" she shouted

I turned and without looking at mother ran up the stairs grateful for being allowed to dress, the following day mother followed up the threat I was dressed in brother's short grey school trousers, and Paul a dress. Mark and June were not subject to this humiliation.

I sat on the curb doodling with a small stone sadness engulfed me for Paul, full of grief and fear that his friends would see him dressed this way; he had hidden in the garden, mother knowing this dragged him through the house to the front door, forcing him out into the front garden in full view of the street, Paul kicked and screamed like he had never done before; this was more distressing to me than my own embarrassment, when this took place he was nearly 15years of age.

Curiosity about my biological father never waned; I yearned for him to rescue me believing he would stop the abuse, scooping me in his arms keeping me protected, and these thoughts kept me going through the bad times. I fantasized reasons for his absence, he had amnesia and would one day gain his memory in time to rescue me, or he was searching for me and had an accident. He was my knight in shinning armour, and the pedestal I placed him on was higher that the tallest building.

I had never been hugged never shown any affection, the only contact I had was physical beatings; the only attention the type that made me feel dirty. Without dreams I would have been lost in myself; I tried hard to stay a good girl hoping Father Arscott would be proud.

I was on the bus with mother when she mentioned father Arscott had been born in a building we just passed, I was fascinated. Perhaps now was the time to ask the questions I desperately wanted answers.

I learned he was called Peter and in the army, he was born in Devon and was re-married, but mother had no idea were he now lived.

"He never wanted any of you." She answered coldly making me feel worthless. Nobody's child I thought, my emotions rising, the hot tears tipping the edge of my eyelids. Bury it deep, don't cry! You don't care I repeated to myself shutting down the pain. Any information I soaked up like a sponge, perhaps he still lived here? I decided to phone every Arscott in the phone directory when nothing was found I phoned the local army barracks and others further away, but I met a dead end. Once again I settled down to the realisation of never finding him, each street I walked I wondered if he had walked the same route, each bus I scanned for some resemblance of me in the faces of strangers.

A few weeks past and I resumed my meagre existence, arriving home from school I noticed someone stood by the gate, realizing it was mother my mind raced,

"What have I done have I been in any trouble? What about school?"

Arms folded and a look that told me I was in real trouble mother motioned me inside. I knew once behind the front door there was no escape.

Hi mum, I greeted in the obsequious tone I always used when I sensed something wrong.

"Don't fucking hi me! Get in doors." mother snarled, teeth clenched.

Frantically searching my mind what could be wrong I had cleaned the house before school, and knew today was Wednesday, mother's half day from work; her being home was nothing out of the norm. I felt as though the black cave had opened up as I stepped inside my prison.

"I will ask you once and once only, who where you trying to phone a few weeks ago?"

No one I whispered, before I could blink she hit me in the face with a clenched fist, the blood spurted from my nose and splattered across her face, my mind racing trying to remember when I had used the phone.

"OH MY GOD, How did they know?" I knew there was no way out I tried to explain I was looking for my dad,

"Why" Step-father interrupted,

"Haven't we done enough for you and your brothers? I take in someone else's bastards and this is how I am repaid."

I was afraid to look them in the eye and worried how to answer their questions, I felt the familiar warm liquid as it trickled down my legs, and was soaked up by my socks and shoes, and I felt belittled even more by my lack of control this happened a lot when they confronted me.

"Get out of my sight you dirty bitch" mother yelled.

I turned to leave but step-father grabbed my arm and forced me to the floor rubbing my face in the urine,

"Animal you dirty fucking bitch"

I was relieved as I climbed the stairs to my room believing it would have been worse, a few hours went by I was unsure whether to go downstairs. I was hungry and could smell the supper cooking; I had dangled my socks and knickers from my bedroom window and dried them for the next day. We only changed our underwear once weekly, on a Sunday. Mother entered my room and sitting on my bed she said we needed to talk,

My biological father had an affair two years before I was born, the woman had a daughter, his daughter, and before I was born the baby died. Mother was sobbing and continued, I was only allowed to keep you if I promised to name you after the dead baby, I refused to give you her second name Victoria, and he took you off me and dumped you and your brothers in an orphanage.

Mother was crying uncontrollably I felt guilty for bringing the painful memories back to her.

"But how did he manage to put us in an orphanage"

She continued to speak and I saw she was agitated by my interruption, he had already left us when you were born, he had many affairs and left us without money, and sometimes food."

I went numb with her rendition of a life with a man I had tried hard to find, she continued to explain.

He asked if he could take all three of us out for the day, mother thought this odd he had not bothered with any of us but gullibly she allowed him. At this point mother was staring out of the window, she had gone very silent almost in a trance, breaking the silence and continuing in a faltering manner.

"It was the right thing for you and I trusted him and thought he would never hurt his children, when he did not return that evening I reported it to the police they found you in the children's orphanage. He took my home from me, we were living in accommodation supplied by the army; I had nowhere to live and no hope of having my children back without able to provide a roof over their heads."

At that moment I felt close to mother she had never spoken in this manner to me, her tone gentle showing a vulnerability that made her appear almost human, for a split second she looked at me with warmth and tenderness in her eyes, some thing else I had not seen.

Mother made me promise never to tell anyone what we had discussed. She walked out of the door and turned to me adding,

"If he ever finds you Sharon, he will have you placed back in care"

I lay on my bed feeling guilty for trying to find him,

What a bastard, how could any man do that to his family? If only I had known good job I never found him. But why does he hate me so much? Why give me some one else's name?"

My last hope of being rescued from the nightmare I lived had just been taken away, deciding to wait until step-father started his night shift, cleaning the local buses, before asking mother for food.

"We are not feeding you," I foolishly believed the conversation we had earlier had changed her.

"Find your real father let him feed you," I was not afraid of mother physically I had come to the conclusion if the fat bastard she was married to could not keep me down, I was able to take anything others dished out, but mental and emotional abuse really hurt, some words mother used bought my self esteem low, believing I was a terrible person.

If they hated me so much why did they not leave me in the orphanage like father Arscott? I believed mother was punishing me for what I accused her husband of; I was desperate for it to stop, and for mother to see the truth.

The following day at school the familiar bruising and the lack of questions, I had a reputation as a troublemaker my attitude in the classroom negative; my behaviour uncontrollable, I didn't bully anyone nor was I bullied, but when things happened at home like the night before, my behaviour in school was appalling, guilt and shame are masters of disguise.

No one cared how I got my bruises the outside world happy to accept what ever tale was told. The time was fast approaching when I would be leaving school; I was going into the armed forces but on applying was informed I had to be least sixteen and a half. Mark was out of the army and living with his girlfriend in the town centre, I had some where to visit when I needed space, I applied for a job in one of the local factories at least I would be earning money, perhaps then I would be able to get a place of my own, leaving this insane existence behind.

But mother insisted I pay three pounds a week out of my wages of seven once I started work.

"We have kept you for nothing these last six years now its time for you to pay us back." mother argued

Hell what about all the money from our paper rounds as soon as our asses hit the pavements of Devon, we were out working our earnings handed over weekly to mother, but as long as they stayed away from me I was willing to pay. Things had got a little easier, I had two more months at school and a job when I finished, and life seemed to be looking up.

The morning of my sixteenth birthday arrived I knew not to expect anything, but this was a special birthday a part of me still hoped this year might be different. Even though Christmas was spent watching June open her presents, it did not seem so terrible when my brothers were home, mother would explain that June's grandparents and aunts had bought the gifts, I had no one who cared enough to buy me.

"You are a nothing you have no one and you belong to no one, Do you realize a piece of fucking wood belongs to some thing; it starts as a tree and ends up being some thing, How do you expect others to want an ugly ass like you? The Ascott's threw you away just as easily as I throw crap in the bin"

These were the usual cruel words used I wish I had the balls to reply,

"And you are the skid Marks on the ass end of society"

Once the front door was closed we became a family of three and an outsider, the horrors unimaginable to any who had not lived through this insanity.

"Happy birthday," Step-father greeted breaking my thoughts. "Thanks Dad," Leaning towards me he whispered in my ear,

"You're of age,"

I knew what he meant he had done some horrific things but had not managed to have full sex, and I knew I would have to be more vigilant.

"Sharon we thought you need your own room now your sixteen and your brothers have gone, It's silly you sharing with June" I didn't want my own room and knew exactly who had manipulated this he knew I was easy prey if I slept alone.

"It's been decided I will start moving your things this morning" Step-father smirked

I walked out of the room and up the stairs blind terror taking over I wanted to scream. I knew there was no way out he had already informed me I was now of age.

"What am I going to do?" June came into the bedroom with a hand made card

"Happy birthday Sharon"

"Thanks June, this is really nice, they want me to have my own bedroom! What do you think?"

"I don't know, Maybe it would be OK."

"I won't be able to sing to you or get into bed with you when you are scared, or tell you stories and draw on your back"

"Tell them you want to stay,"

"You tell them, go on tell them you want me to stay with you."

I listened as June informed her parents and went back downstairs to be told that mother had changed her mind; the spare room should be left just in case my brothers returned. I felt smug realizing I could be just as manipulative, I had won this battle but the war was still raging, for the first time in a long while I had a spring in my step, I was sixteen today and outwitted the night devil.

I was saddened to be leaving school but prepared, it was a small step in my plans to escape the claws of my abusers. The weeks ticked by and the beatings became less, I was quick to fight off the perverted advances of step-father during my waking hours, but at night he still visited, some times I would wake with no knowledge of his nightly visit, the only signs visible were my night clothes pulled down, I was thankful I had no memory of the nights events and believed the night June screamed waking mother, was the night the bastard was almost caught.

Believing she saw a ghost standing over my bed her screams woke the whole house, step-father was exiting the bedroom as mother arrived, pretending he just got there mother did not seek to find why he was naked. I noticed he had a tattoo on his ass I think a sea creature, I am not sure but the octopus tattooed on his back I fantasized many times had come alive and choked the bastard to death.

"I am going to Canada in a few months time; would you like to come Sharon?"

I excitedly accepted the invitation I was starting work tomorrow so could afford it.

"You save your spending money, and I will pay your air fare" This was more than I could ever hope from mother; to be included in a holiday was thrilling.

"Then you will have to pay five pounds a week lodging to cover the amount for you ticket is that OK?"

I hesitated slightly, that would leave me two pounds to save for spending money, and other things I need

"It's up to you; don't say you were not asked."

"Is Dad going with us?"

"No."

"OK, I will go." A few weeks passed and all I could think about was the holiday next year,

I am off to Canada in three weeks time and have picked up the tickets this morning." Mother informed as I entered the house after work, I was dumbfounded it was only three weeks ago she invited me.

"I will have to inform work I can't just take a month off I will lose my job."

"You're not going," mother snapped I thought it was a joke I couldn't begin to accept being in the house alone with the night devil.

"Why mum"

"Because you have no spending money you have not tried hard enough to save."

I pleaded and begged for her to change her mind," Don't leave me here not on my own."

"You won't be alone your dad will be here."

Silence fell I could find no words, had she deliberately done this? It would not be the first time she had messed with my mind.

"Don't be so bloody selfish you fucking bitch." Mother started to shout

"You have made no effort to save and you are not sponging off me for a month, your dad's right you need to be taught a lesson, life is not a bed of roses and you have to earn life's luxuries." I wanted to scream in her face, my life has always been a bed of fucking roses, only some bastard nicked my petals and left the thorns, he will hurt me if you go but knew this was pointless, mother became aggressive but this time I was ready had she lifted her hand to hit me I believe I would have fought her physically.

The day came for mother and June to board the train for the airport, standing on the platform watching the train disappear from view; I wanted to throw myself on the tracks.

"Come on I am going to the pub for a drink, you coming with me?"

"No thanks" I was smiling at him trying to keep him in a happy mood.

"I have promised to see Sara I will catch the bus back, you go on Dad, and I will see you at home"

I rushed away disappearing into the mass of people; walking to the beach I tried to gather my thoughts. If only I knew Paul's address in Scotland, I could have gone there for a few weeks. But no one had heard from him since he had left the navy eight months ago.

Sitting on the bench it did not matter the weather was wet and windy; I buried my head in my hands and started to cry, I felt there was nothing left for me to fight with. I started homewards I was going to get through the next month the best way I could, and not worry about any thing until it happened.

Later that evening I phoned step-father and made excuses for not returning. I was desperate for some one to talk to, to share my sordid secret; I decided not to stay in the house alone with him returning only when I watched his car leave the street. Sleeping at various friend's houses, and visiting Mark and his girlfriend, this was to work well. I was happy with my life at present and feared no one it had been one week of bliss even though some nights were spent under the stars; I bumped into three of my friends,

"Where are you going?"

"Jim has found a way into the brewery he is going to wheel some barrels down the field to us, you coming?"

"Try stopping me" I jumped at the chance just to be with some one, it would also help the time pass, the weekend was upon me and I had no work for two days, my work mates all went out on the town Friday nights. I had nothing to wear and no money, step-father was still making me pay five pounds lodge which I left on the kitchen side for him.

Making our way to the local woods we got our selves settled into different groups, each group of ten teenagers sat in the large craters that had been left from the last war. I could not believe how many had turned up.

"There must be twenty kids here Sharon, do you want a ciggy"

"Thanks, Bobby-Joe I was trying to give them up but I am finding it hard, wish I never started"

"Why did you start? You've not been smoking long have you?"

"My mother slapped the shit out of me a few months ago, said some one told her I was smoking so I thought up yours bitch. I might as well do what I am being hit for, went to school the following morning and lit my first one, regretted it ever since"

There was a noise like thunder and it was getting nearer,

"Oh bloody hell there are horses in the field and it sounds like they are stampeding" Jerry shouted.

Every one started to panic; straining to see in the dark

I stood up in time to see a barrel pass gathering speed. A chorus of laughter broke out amongst the groups,

"Get ready to catch another one, it's coming down" Jim shouted to all. Whoosh… that also shot past gathering speed and smashing onto the rocks on the edge of the woods below.

"Try another it was to dark to see that one" Bobby-Joe called back

"When I say now I am going to let another roll down,"

"NOW" he shouted loudly,

Bobby-Joe and I got ready to catch the rolling barrel,

"Tony you have the screw driver you open it"

Tony chipped away until the beer spilled out like a fountain soaking us all.

"I thought beer barrels were made of wood not metal"

"Yes Jerry you also thought they were fucking horses," Bobby-Joe teased,

We all laughed I was a little apprehensive about drinking alcohol, but after a few sips began to relax.

"Your old lady's away for a while Sharon, is that why you are here" Jim asked

"She is away but that has nothing to do with me being here"

"Oh it's just you are never out at night usually"

"Oh I see what you mean she doesn't stop me going any where, I just never wanted to do this before"

I lied, trying to sound matter of fact.

"Who's coming to help me get some more barrels?"

Jerry, Anita, Fay, and I decided to go making our way to the brewery I knew what we were doing was wrong, but the buzz electrifying.

"Take what we need now, save coming back" I liked belonging to a gang and the camaraderie that bound us together.

"Yeah good idea might as well there's enough of us," Jim agreed. I felt excited about the illegal activity, the adrenaline rush getting me high and the beer made me feel a little braver.

We wheeled seven more barrels but only managed to drink half a barrel between us the others hidden in bushes for another night. We swaggered to the small park and sat on the swings and generally mucked about, for a few hours I was able to forget the troubles at home

"Where are you sleeping tonight?"

"In the woods loads of us sleep here when we can get the booze, that way our old dears don't find out we have been drinking, what about you?"

"I will stay with you if that's ok" this was the most relaxed I had been in a long time I sat back on the swing, and just enjoyed the moment.

I managed to stay clear of step-father, only occasionally bumping into him seeing each other only as he came in the house and I Leaving. My days spent working and my nights down the local woods drinking. Perhaps he has changed I pondered, he had made no attempts to frighten me or to touch, I returned at six o'clock in the evening after he had left a note the day before explaining he was to work early. I was happy to return at that hour to have a bath and just relax.

I entered the house and immediately knew he was still there, I could smell the stale odour of beer.

"I thought you said you where working early tonight?"

"No, it's about time you spent some time at home," he replied.

"I am baby-sitting for Mark and Linda, I can't let them down I have already said I will do it."

"I am off for a drink and will be back later tonight."

Relief swept through me as I locked all the windows and doors and started to run the bath. I had not bathed at home since mother left; not wanting to provoke him in any way, now was the perfect time securing the house making sure no one would be able to enter, not even with a key. The downstairs curtains drawn closed I felt protected, as I entered the bath the phone started ringing it was step-father informing me he would be later than expected. Explaining the police were looking over his car, he would be at least an hour I believed him he always drove whilst drunk and probably does to this day.

Making a mug of tea I preceded to the bathroom sliding into the water I heard a key in the front door lock.

"No! It can't be!" my mind racing who could it be, it was impossible to be step-father he had just phoned and said he was a good sixty minutes away.

"Who is it?" I shouted whilst rushing to get dressed

"It's me Open the fucking door" Step-father replied.

I was in frenzy how did he get home so quick he started banging on the bathroom window.

"Open the bloody door!"

I raced into the kitchen and gathering my clothes I saw him looking through the window the v shape at the top of the curtains gave him enough of a gap to see in.

Oh! My God I have to get out the house before he gets in; I knew the bastard had tricked me I had to get out.

"Go to the back door dad I will open it."

I ran to the front door and dressed quickly in the privacy of the small passage, he was banging on the lounge window shouting for me to open the door, his frustration obvious by the tone in his voice as quietly as I could I opened the front door stepping into the garden and yelling.

"The front doors open I have to rush, Mark has just phoned and I am running late, Bye."

I jumped over the front fence and dashed out of the street, once again sleeping in the local woods.

I felt safe there; the beatings had stopped since I started work although the mental abuse hadn't, the next few days I spent at my brother's.

"Tomorrow mother is home,"

"Have you missed her?" Linda asked.

"Yes, like a fucking hole in the head" I mocked, the truth was I had not, but rather the security of her presence

step-father was working tonight I felt a certain pride I had outsmarted him, returning home at ten o'clock in the evening. The house would be empty and step-father would have started his night shift at the local bus-cleaning depot. I put my key in the lock and felt uneasy walking into the lounge; step-father appeared from the kitchen.

"What are you doing home? I thought you were working tonight"

My mind racing for an excuse to leave the house again

"I do live here as well you know,"

I went straight to my room and paced the floor wondering what he was doing downstairs, I was angry I had become smug, I didn't wait long instinct told me I was in trouble, and again he had tricked me into believing he was working. He was climbing the stairs heading for my room, jumping up onto the windowsill fight or flight time had arrived, I knew he was going to rape me, there was no one to stop this, no one to hear my cries. Looking down onto the garden below I was afraid to jump, the door opened he was standing in my room completely naked. I had not been prepared for this, scanning the room in a frantic haze of tears.

"Don't come any closer," This was the worst fear I had ever felt I wanted to shut off close my eyes and fall of the ledge.

"I will jump." I threatened

"Don't be a dumb bitch, and get the fuck down," he sneered. "You will break your neck if you jump or your legs, yes go jump if you're fucking legs brake you cant fucking run"

I knew he was right was I willing to take that chance, I was angry with myself for allowing him to trick me, he snatched Molly Dolly from my bed and threatened to break her, I was horrified but not about to give in for the sake of a Doll.

"Are you for fucking real?" I screamed

He took a step towards me and I could see the annoyance in his face.

"I swear to God I will jump you mother fucker," I screamed as loud as I possible could, hoping some one would hear and knock the door.

"I have all night; your ass will be mine by the nights hour bitch"

He pulled Molly's head off throwing it at me and proceeded to snap off her arms, tossing them behind him and sneering. Lifting her remains above his head and throwing her straight at me, she bounced out the window and onto the garden below, leaving my room his laughter echoing through the stairwell, I knew he was right somehow I have to get out of the house.

I looked below for Molly but dusk had settled and the darkness engulfing all that was left of her. If I jump and hurt my leg I would be stuck, he would drag me back into the house. I would be totally defenceless against him, talking through different solutions cautiously analyzing each, knowing I would only have one chance and if I failed, I knew in my heart he would raped me. I could hear him moving around downstairs and knew it was no good trying to pretend this was not happening, I only had my self to rely.

Oh I wish I had turned the bloody light on I could wait for some one to see me it was past eleven, my only light the full moon which shone bright, opening up the dark corners of my room. I needed to barricade myself in I looked around there was no furniture, accept two single beds, and he would hear me dragging them across the floor.

OK. OK. Think, stay calm. I had sat with my legs dangling from the window for nearly three hours, they were going numb, and the sill was starting to embed into the backs of my legs. I decided to wait until he was asleep and then sneak out the house.

Barricading my self in was my only option placing both beds, end to end against the door was a good idea; I moved my legs around trying and get some feeling back into them before I dropped back to the floor. Tiptoeing across the floor hardly daring to put my weight behind my step, and very gently lifting my bed at one end, carefully swinging it towards the door getting it in place, swiftly closing the door I heard him rushing up the stairs, the bastard had heard me no time left I slammed the bed in front of the door and sat with my back to the wall holding my feet rigid on the bed frame. Nothing was going to get into that room; he would have to break my legs.

He started to threaten, trying to scare me into opening the door then talking nicely, explaining he was playing that I needed to stop being silly; he was going to tell mother how stupid I had been. I never answered his pleas and sat in the dark all night holding the bed in place with my feet, too afraid to relax, too afraid to sleep. The night devil was still behind my bedroom door,

"Pst come and get it you know you want to, you little prick teaser" he jeered me and continued his vile renditions of what he was going to do with my body, I placed my hands over my ears and started to hum gently, how had it got to this what had I done that gave him the idea I liked living this way. Mother would be home in several hours and I knew I was in big trouble for swearing at step-father, but hell I enjoyed it.

Oh god what's he doing now my ears straining to find out what was going on beyond the bedroom door. I had lost myself in my own daydream. I heard him entering his room and his bed creak as his large frame slumped onto it.

"I CAN WAIT BITCH, I love it when you tease me with your little games of catch me if you can." he taunted.

I stayed silent with visions of him getting an axe and chopping down the door, or setting fire to the house as he already threatened earlier, if I goaded him with a reply, my imagination scarring the shit out of me.

Many hours had passed I had time to reflect many things that night, and was going to tell mother everything, listening to him snoring in the next room I decided it was time to make a dash for freedom. The dawn was breaking and bright sunshine gleamed into my room, my legs heavy and stiff I noticed my precious Molly Dolly's arms in the corner of the room and felt immense pain, it was as though I had lost a friend, my Molly had been through every thing with me from the age of four to present day, how I wish she were able to speak. I had to try and leave the house now; I may not get another chance and knew the fat bastard would be in a deep sleep after drinking.

What if he was only pretending to be asleep, my mind started to race again; fear was stopping me from plucking up the courage to leave. Lifting my legs I needed to get the blood flowing again each in turn I moved, until they started to feel less weak. Sliding the bed away from the door I gradually opened it nervously listening for any sign of him waking, knowing I had to take it slowly.

Creeping along the narrow landing I could hear him snoring reaching the top stair certain he could hear my breathing, gradually I started the descent down. Each step creaked louder than the last making me stop and listen, the front door now in sight safety lay beyond. I remember the last time he caught me unaware on these stairs, his feral look burned into my memory I was scaring myself with memories of bygone days, of beatings and abuse. Wanting desperately to rush but afraid the front door would not open, I flicked the catch and unbolted the locks and slowly opened the door.

The cold morning air swirled around my face as I started to run, leaving the door of my prison wide open. I had no idea where I was going but where ever it was it had to be better then what I had left. I was free! I was running in blind panic, inside my head a storm was brewing.

Giggling and laughing and then crying, there was no controlling it; hearing the most horrendous scream it was a few seconds before I realized it was I.

It was six thirty in the morning and I needed to stay off the main roads afraid he would come looking, The morning air was fresh with a biting feel to it a clean fresh feeling ran through my body, I had won the fat bastard it was going to be a glorious sunny day. Nine o'clock I decided to call on Rosie, a good friend whom I had known for three years.

"Good God you look awful."

"Is there somewhere private we can talk?"

"Yes sure we can talk here I have the house to myself, Come in"

I had decided to tell Rosie everything

"I can't believe it; he always seemed so nice you will have to tell your mother Sharon!"

I explained what had happened the last time mother was told; it was a relief sharing all that had happened with another.

"Promise me you won't tell anyone what I have just told you,"

"I promise, but you can't go on like this Sharon, you have to get help."

"I am going to tell mother everything If I don't he is going to hurt me, I will meet her later at the train station."

"You can stay here all day if you like,"

The day went in a blur but the time spent allowed me to come to a very important decision, no matter what was said or done, he was not going to hurt me any more,

"I don't know how I will do it Rosie, some how with Gods help and a lot of luck" I joked, trying to sound positive.

The time was upon me to catch the bus to the train station I played in my mind what I was going to say, rehearing my speech over and over. I would not back down this time and stand my ground if he tried to deny any of it and make me look the liar, I was getting off the bus and heard someone shouting

"About time too," I looked around and saw step-father approaching, I was shocked by his attitude or rather lack of it.

"Where have you been?"

I could not believe the way he was acting it was as though last night never happened, I had kept out of sight all day terrified he was going to kill me, and here we were as though the fat bastard was eligible for parent of the year award. Walking towards the platform

I could see mother and June getting off the train. The fat bastard ran towards them I held back and watched the family reunion, it was as though I did not exist, mother would not believe me and the fat bastard was not going to stop until he got what he wanted.

The car journey home was purgatory for me listening to the talk of a holiday filled with sunshine laughter and joy, I informed mother I was baby-sitting for Mark, no one batted an eye lid, we arrived outside the house and I looked to the front door. Last night seemed a life time away I was never a part of their family; no one gave a second thought as they entered the house leaving me on the pavement, I felt like an entity visiting an old life. I was totally numb and tired of constantly being on guard, last night had taken its toll I needed sleep, focusing on any thing was hard. Most teenagers my age fantasized about their first sexual encounter, I dreaded it to the point of insanity.

❧ Chapter Seven ❧

I watched as a friendly figure approached, it was Rosie; I was pleased to see a friend, inviting her to come along to Marks house linking arms we walked towards the bus stop. Talking about the day's events my goodness this was strange, being able to talk to another and not myself. I had changed my mind again and decided not to tell mother.

A car horn beeped loudly behind us it was step-father, Rosie tightened her grip on my arm, he opened the passenger door and told us to get in, and he was going to give us a lift. I knew I would be OK, Rosie was with me but slightly concerned why he had come after us I got in the front and Rosie the back. He tried to make conversation but his mere presence making my skin crawl, I had a real urge to scream at him, a hateful anger over whelming me it frightened me to feel this way, some thing had changed within me I had no clue what it was, but my attitude and feelings towards this animal sat besides me was of contempt, rather than fear.

Relieved when our destination was reached opening the car door step-father grabbed my arm squeezing tightly, I slumped besides him on the front seat.

"Keep your mouth shut about last night"

The expressions on his face made any thoughts of me standing up to him melt away, who was I kidding this asshole scared the shit out of me.

"Yes I will dad" I pitifully squirmed hating myself for cowering down to the animal.

"You had better because if you don't I will kill you and anyone you tell." He gestured towards Rosie with his eyes and I knew exactly what he meant, but I also knew this was an idle threat I was beginning to realize what a coward he really was, I was an easy target for this bully but Rosie had her families backing, I scrambled out of the car and he drove off,

"I heard what that bastard said, you have to tell some one."

"I can't no one will believe me,"

I calmed Rosie down she became hysterical believing he was going to hurt her; I couldn't really deal with hysteria and wanted to tell her to go home. But I needed to calm her and make sure she kept her mouth shut, I wished with all my heart I had never told her.

We entered Linda's home and I offered my services for baby-sitting, trying to sound cheerful and unafraid.

"Bloody hell Rosie you ok? You look as though you have seen a ghost"

"Hi Linda I will be ok just had a few things happen these past few days" Rosie sat in the corner I was worried about her she seemed over anxious about the car incident, I shot a menacing stare in her direction trying to burn my thoughts into her brain. Linda joked about my time spent there the last month and we made small talk about mothers return. I got the impression Linda disliked mother, but she never openly admitted it.

"Your brothers couldn't wait to leave we are surprised you are still there,"

I always felt guilty wondering if I had done something to provoke step-father, I was finding it hard to feel emotion apart from anger, and if I left where would I go. I had no one and nowhere the conversation was making me feel even angrier. Knowing Linda was right made my guilt more consuming, why had I not left home I was allowing things to happen the disgrace engulfing me.

"Well one thing's for sure I would have hit the bastards back and no one would do to me what they have done to you three."

"Tell her Sharon; tell Linda what he has done"

I snapped at Rosie to shut her mouth, if looks could kill she would have breathed her last breath.

"What's going on?"

Quietness circled the room as we all looked to each other I grabbed Rosie's arm and pulled her out to the courtyard.

"I think you need to tell some one I heard what he said when you were getting out the fucking car."

Rosie was starting to get hysterical again, she had never experienced anything like this and his threats to kill any that knew my grubby secret, was too much for her to cope with.

"What if he finds out that you told me?"

"Don't be so fucking stupid he won't come after you I won't tell him I have told you,"

My anger surging towards her believing she was a selfish asshole, and only wanting to reveal every thing to save her sorry ass.

"What the hell is going on" Linda appeared she was getting anxious with the conversation and my attitude towards Rosie.

"Oh! Its just Rosie, over reacting dad went to hit me and missed, he said he would sort me out when I get home but he does not want to spoil Mother's home-coming."

"What the fuck are you doing? Stop lying" Rosie screamed frantically.

"Doing what someone had better start telling me what the hell you two are talking about." Linda cut in.

"You are talking in riddles."

I grabbed her arm and shoved her towards the gate trying to force her to leave with me, faced with this confrontation I wanted to leave, pulling away from me she re-entered the house and sat at the table, I followed wanting to silence this weak idiot my anger welling fearing what she would say.

"Sharon calm down I will put the kettle on go for a walk or something" Linda advised.

I stormed out of the house and sat on the pavement I was angry with myself for confiding in Rosie. It had been one of my weakest moments, returning to Linda's home I heard the whispered tones of their voices deep in conversation, and I listened enough to know she was telling her every thing.

My life was a mess why hadn't mother believed me the first time he touched me, I got out of the house quickly uncertain how to react, walking slowly deep in thought I was scared of the coming few hours. I would have to call her a liar or tell the truth, I could see no reason for living it seemed death was my only option.

I wondered aimlessly and my mind frenzied with worry either way I am a dead person by means of suicide, mother, or step-father, cupping my face I started to sob I was in the wilderness of loneliness the only way out is to end my life; I started walking towards the heavy traffic.

Just close your eyes and keep walking the traffic was getting louder and a few more steps should do it, a loud horn bellowed through the air I nearly peed my pants it scared me witless, opening my eyes the truck driver was giving me the v sign, and swearing loudly some one calling my name bought me out of my deep abyss of thought.

It was Linda she had come looking and was very angry and upset; she had witnessed me walking towards the traffic and screamed out for me to stop. I did not hear her and was not sure if her calling would have been enough to stop me. For the first time I could not look her in the eye, I believed if she saw into my eyes she would see what had been done to me over the years, shame fear and facing up to the past six years was over bearing. We walked at a snail's pace towards her home without a word spoken; entering the kitchen Rosie looked up towards me, I blamed her for this her and her mouth.

"You need to go to the police,"

"What for what lies has she told you?"

"Rosie has told me everything wait till your brother comes home from work he should be here about eleven tonight."

I did not want Mark to know, and begged them to forget the events of that evening, I knew I could not deny it and make Rosie out to be a liar, but they failed to understand the shame I felt.

"I am going home I'm sorry for telling Linda, but when you left I needed to tell some one."

"I should never have told you I am so scared what's going to happen to me."

Rosie hugged me, this was the first time any one had shown me compassion,

"What ever is ahead is better than what you have left"

I knew Rosie was right and although I feared having to face the judgment of my brother, I was also relieved it was finally out in the open.

When my brother returned home Linda took him into the kitchen and explain the night's events, I was not prepared for the reaction, he did not believe me!

He fired questions at an alarming rate how long had it been going on? Why had I not told some one? You could have stopped it! All these things he was shouting.

"Fear!"

I shouted back, would you have helped me? NO! Remember when I did tell mother the first time he touched me, she beat me up, no one believed me then."

I was angry, humiliated and saddened by Marks attitude towards me I needed his support more than anyone's.

"I don't remember that," Mark bellowed

"You don't remember very much you've always had selective memory?"

"We need to ask some one how we go about reporting this mother will know what to do"

The decision was made to go immediately to Linda's mother's home; Pam did not like our parents, Linda relayed things Mark had told her about his past, Pam found it difficult to imagine anyone treating a child this way.

She listened to what Linda had to say, I could not bring myself to talk to anyone about it

"I am going to phone the police"

I felt as though I was losing control last night only I knew what was going on, now everyone seemed to know I felt dirty and cheap was I in trouble for allowing it to go on? At the police station I was interviewed by a male officer I found this uncomfortable.

I was not at ease going into detail about past events with another man. The guilt I had carried was reinforced by the attitudes of the officers, I felt as though they were stripping me bare of any respect I may have retained. There searching questions and lack of decorum pushed me further from my own reality of events.

They wanted dates, I could not give dates, they wanted times; I could not give those either, I knew the first time he touched me and the events surrounding it, and also the last time in explicit detail, but anything else in between was all mixed into each other. Trying to explain the sexual abuse had been mainly at night, when the house was still.

No, I had no idea what time of night it was, No, I had never called out. All this questioning was making me feel I deserved what happened.

Yes I had told him No, on many occasions, yes, I had told someone before, mother, but she disbelieved. A continued onslaught of questions that provoked disgusting images in my head, metaphors I had buried and descriptions I had learned to flee from, similes that were rocking my world with humiliation. There reactions reinforced my guilt I pleaded with them to speak to mother.

"Mother will verify what I have told you, mother could give the date of the first time, it was when she went on holiday with my sister June."

After many hours I was allowed to leave the police station I was advised they were going to arrest step-father and not to return home until they had time to go to my home.

Returning to my brother's house I was terrified of bumping into step-father, he was not going to be happy.

My brother was waiting for my return and I asked that I stay there for a few days, they were arresting step-father and once he tells them why he did what he has, he will be removed from the home. I felt sorry for mother she was about to find out what a pig her husband was. Envisioning her arms around me as she repeats how sorry she is for not believing me.

"You can't stay here"

"Where am I supposed to go?"

"I don't know but I don't want the fat bastard here threatening us."

"Mother said you could stay at her home for a while, if that will help"

I thanked Linda but the hurt I felt towards my brother was stronger than anything I had felt before.

I truly believed mother would do what was right it didn't occur to me people would lie to the police.

I moved into Pam's house and shared a room with three other girls, a week later I was asked to attend the police station. I was again asked to go through the events of the past six years, they had interviewed my night devil who had denied all charges, and we don't feel the need for you to have a medical you have stated you have not had full sex with him"

I felt my world collapsing I was uncomfortable with this male officer talking to me, and I could feel all my emotions surfacing, I wanted to cry and scream but all I did was giggle. Desperately I tried to control the urge to laugh, but could no longer contain it. I felt as though I was being abused all over again.

"How many boyfriends have you had?"

"I have never had a boyfriend"

"How many have you slept with?"

He asked again, ignoring my answer to his first question,

"None,"

"So you are asking us to believe a pretty girl like yourself has never had a boyfriend?

I would not kiss a boy he always chased off any potential boyfriends whether I was interested or not.

Why did you not scream when he was holding you down in the lounge, his manner condescending and judgmental?

I felt guilty for not seeking help earlier; I wanted to scream at them,

I could not scream in the lounge for fear of him forcing me into oral sex, scenes of violence and violation surged through my mind at an alarming rate, I no longer heard them speaking I was transported back to the house and remembering minuet details, I tried switching off the pain but my images were like a video fast winding.

"Would you consent to a medical?

"What is a medical? What would I have to do?"

The officer explained the procedure I was horrified, but felt I had no choice and agreed.

"Why are you asking me all these questions?"

"Your mother informed us you sleep around and on many occasions you have attended your doctor making sure you were not pregnant."

"She's lying, yes I have been to the doctor's nearly every month but I have never slept with anyone, my doctor can tell you this."

I swallowed hard I was not going to show them I was upset, I was starting to see the police as my enemy, the lies mother had told and the condemnatory way this officer was talking confounded me.

"So your doctor examined you on many occasions and can verify this?"

"No I was never examined he just asked me things about what I had done, and a reason for my periods being late, have you spoken to my dad? Has he told you everything?"

"He has denied everything in fact you often lied to gain attention.

"I am telling you the truth"

"Did you ever tell anyone else?"

"Yes I told Rosie after the night I hid in my room, Up until then I had only told mother, but she did not believe me."

I was starting to realize the enormity of the situation, the police were going to speak to Rosie and they would take it from there, they would be in touch.

Leaving the police station I felt totally exhausted my head spinning with the day's events, it was one o'clock in the afternoon and I had been at the station since nine that morning. Making my way to the local beach I sat deep in thought and contemplation of a future I was sure existed.

It was not supposed to be like this, I had no home, no family, not even a change of clothes, I was desperate for someone to believe me, one by one people were disappearing from my life distancing them selves from the twisted hateful Sharon. I thought of ways to get step-father to tell the truth, taking a tape recording of him threatening me, fantasizing he would tell the truth maybe a lie detecting machine would help, surely some one or thing could prove what I had said.

I hate him, I am homeless a tramp, I was filled with dread, the full reality was starting to unfold this is not suppose to be like this, he is suppose to be punished for doing what he has done I was still confused why I was homeless and he not in prison, what he did was wrong my head was swimming in a quagmire of hurt and confusion.

I had been sitting for eight hours and it was getting dark I watched the sun going down it looked like a big orange balloon, I could almost hear it sizzle as it appeared to tip the waters, and sink below the horizon that stretched out before me, I likened it to my own existence. This immersed me into a depressing thought of desolation, but as the moon rose in all its glory it gave me hope for new days ahead. Starting the long silent walk home I noticed the moon following me, imagining a guardian angel lighting my path. Suddenly I realized there was no one to miss me I could disappear forever, be murdered and no one would know.

Standing at Pam's gate I was aware this was my life from now on,

"How did you get on" Pam asked with her inquiring mind. What I needed was someone to hold me, to tell me all would be OK and to take this burden away. Inside I was dying, my heart heavy; someone saying they believed me would make a difference, I explained they were to speak with Rosie again.

"Have they said when it will go to court?"

"What do you mean court?"

"You will have to go to court if he keeps denying it,"

No way was I going to stand in a room full of strangers and go into detail what he had done to me; I had not really given the full details I was ashamed and could not find the strength or the right way to explain. As for a courtroom I had only seen one on the TV.

What had I done, I should have kept my mouth shut what if I told the police it was all lies? I could go back home it was not so bad? I had coped before. step-father would not touch me again he would know I would report it, yes that's what I will do, tomorrow I will go to the police station and tell them it was all a mistake.

I got ready bright and early the following morning I was starting to have nightmares, where once my dreams were a safe escape from the horrors around me, now they were nightmares filled with pictures of step-father's face as he invaded my dreams.

In my nightmares I can neither run nor shout, some times I am not aware of what chases me I only know it terrifies. My second dream less dramatic but still worrisome, I dream of flying up and away over the rooftops and far away, I wake trembling with fear.

Over and over in my mind rehearsing what I will say, approaching the inquiry desk I asked for Detective Morrison. I ask myself what the hell I am doing here am I really doing the right thing, If I go home after telling them I lied he will be able to do anything he pleases.

Mother lied, why? She must have known what was going on if not, why would she lie about me having sex with others? My bloody head was spinning with all the unanswered questions.

If I lied to the police now I would be allowing him to get away with it walking towards the door I hesitate

No, I am doing the right thing people will believe me the truth always comes out in the end; even the night devil would not be able to fool a judge. I was starting to sort things out for myself I may not have been loved as a daughter should, but I was a human being and was important to me. I wished there was some one to talk to about the feelings running around in my head, feelings of self-harm, anger for allowing him to manipulate, and extreme rage for trusting people around me. Believing I would be helped naive enough to believe mother would protect, that the authorities would stop him.

Step-father should be punished not me, his life had not changed apart from me accusing the fat bastard of abuse, I was destitute no family it was as though the past six years had never happened. Puff! All gone as quick as a snap of the fingers telling the truth don't always pay.

Every one was telling me I was doing the right thing, none of them were going to stand by my side openly telling others they believed me. Society had turned on me for dare objecting, for daring to say no more, I returned to Pam's house and waited to hear from the police. I was going to try and stay positive, with out it negativity would take over and I was not sure if mentally I would survive. As the days past I became more depressed and started to drink to help numb my pain, I was able to forget my true feelings when inebriated. I stopped eating and withdrew from the outside world, fearing bumping into mother or the night devil. I no longer had a job and Pam was allowing me to stay purely for the need to know what was going on. It seemed a lifetime since the police had called; deeper and deeper I sank into depression and low self worth.

Watching the wildlife films shown on the television, the pride of lions make the kill, the scavengers eating the bones to pick the carcass clean. The lions depict my family the scavengers my friends and neighbours, the kill myself

"There's a phone call for you, it's the police." Pam called, after speaking for a few minutes I placed the receiver down and could see Pam's need to know the conversation that had passed.

"They asked I attend the station tomorrow hopefully I will be going home"

"You would go back and live with him after all you have said?"

"No not with step-father, no way, I mean once they charge him he will have to leave the house"

Once again I started the familiar walk to the police station; I had never been in trouble with the police but was starting to know the station very well.

I was asked to wait they would be with me shortly, the suspense of the outcome to their inquiries was overwhelming, I starting making mental images of a family reunion in my mind, I was led into a room Detective Morrison tried to explain the situation

"There is not enough evidence to prosecute,"

"Have you spoken to Rosie? She will tell you what I said to her"

"She has no knowledge of the situation she has retracted the statement she originally made"

"Why? Why would she lie what the hells wrong with every body what are you all so bloody afraid off?" my anger rising.

"Calm down Sharon"

"Don't you dare tell me to calm down look at me for Christ sakes, what did I ever do?"

"Had he been your real father then perhaps we could have proceeded."

I could contain my feeling no longer and the tears flowed, anger, fear, distress, all rolled into one I was let down by all who were involved, and disappointed most of all no one believed, he had got away with all the abuse and like he had said many times, no one cared.

Detective Morrison walked me to the front entrance I felt like I was being thrown back into the lion's den, the world was a cruel place to live if you were sixteen had been savagely abused and had no one to turn to.

"I wish there was some thing we could do Sharon, if he had raped you then in a sad way it would have helped."

I looked up to him and thought how I had put my faith and trust in the truth, always believing good will overcome evil.

"If he had raped me then you would be looking for a body"

"Good luck Sharon" he added

As I walked through the door I turned and looked into his eyes I believe the eyes are the windows to our souls, they tell you a lot about a person. I saw a kind genuine person I put my hand up to stop the door closing.

"One more thing, he did all I told you and more, every thing I have told you is the way it was" I turned and left not giving him time to answer.

Reaching the bottom step I looked back to the door, he had gone. He was now investigating another crime and would soon forget me, but I on the other hand would never forget him.

Returning to Pam's home Mark, was waiting he already knew the outcome he had been to mothers home and they where celebrating.

"Why did you do it?"

"You don't believe me do you?"

"Come on how can anyone allow that to go on as long as you say it did?"

How could I possibly answer that question when I couldn't understand, I was still a child trying to cope alone in an adult world with adult problems, and facing the judgment from all around.

"You are my brother Mark; do you really believe I could make up such terrible lies?"

"I know I never saw anything like what you say went on, mother says it's because you have always wanted our real dad"

"You can all piss off Mark"

"No, you piss off no one wants you here you're a lying bitch" he snapped

How dare he judge me, how dare mother lie reality was dawning the pipe dream of a happy family reunion was all it was, a pipe dream, Mark stormed out of Pam's house.

I shouted after him

"Just because none of you believe me don't mean it never happened" I rushed upstairs and sobbed into my pillow, I had lost everything. I knew step-father would come after me I knew him better than any, disbelieving me only made it easier for him to hurt me again, if I was ever sure of one thing in my entire life, I was sure it was not over. But there was some one who would have to explain them selves to me, Rosie, she had lied to the police I am going to hurt her bad.

That bitch had cost me greatly, searching the streets I was determined to find her, catching sight of her outside Gloria's gate,

"What do you think you are playing at you bitch?" I screamed lunging at her

"You bastard, I am going to kill you why? You bastard, I thought you were my friend" Rosie screamed terrified of my rage.

"My mother made me change my statement I had no choice please Sharon, don't hurt me, please"

Rosie's indisputable fear snapped me out of my rage I saw myself in my friend's eyes and the unmistakable terror from the beating she thought I was going to dish out, releasing my grip we both flopped to the floor exhausted.

"Why Rosie, just tell me why you lied"

"My old dear made me change my first statement, your mother came and saw her the other night and told my mother you were bullying me to lie for you"

Rosie continued to explain her mother was scared step-father would get angry with them, she don't want to get involved Rosie was told to stay away from me, I was bad news

"But you know the fucking truth you saw him threaten me you only have to tell the truth, I would do it for you"

I begged like I had never begged before but to no avail, Rosie was more afraid of her parents than telling the truth, who could blame her. I never saw Rosie again and became more withdrawn from every day life. I neither bathed nor changed what little clothing I had, and during my waking hours I would be looking around every corner, living in dread of step-father.

It had been two months since I was informed no more would be done, walking back from the shops I noticed a white van slowing down on the opposite side of the road, I was not concerned the van did a u-turn in the middle of the road, and instinctively I started to run as it reversed, screeching its tyres along the tarmac, blind panic took over as I saw step-fathers sneering face at the wheel. When I accused him of chasing me or shouting threats from across the street, others accused me of paranoia the time had come for me to leave Devon.

Too many people were eager to judge, too many willing to give an opinion on something they knew nothing about, as with all council estates news spreads fast I had lost a lot of friends because of the accusations. People did not want their child associated with someone who could make up such stories about a man who was well liked within the community, mother had called me a liar and publicly supported the fat bastard, and mothers don't do that, do they?

No one had thought to question why step-father or mother had never confronted me; some one accused falsely of such a serious crime surely would want to know why.

Why on mothers return home from a month away did he leave the house within minutes of her arrival to give me a lift. Some times silence speaks volumes, the second time he chased me was the last straw. I was in our local rubbish dump good pickings were to be had if you got there early enough. I had learnt where there's muck there's brass, and I needed as much money as possible to leave this god forsaken existence I had slipped into.

Remembering my brothers and I used to come to the rubbish tip regular for step-father, he would send us looking for any old scraps of metal, selling it for his beer money. I noticed some one approaching me they were waving, I smiled and waved back wondering who the heck my friend was. To my horror realizing it was the night devil the bastard had a hat on, his face obstructed from view he started to run towards me and as I turned I caught my foot in the rubbish beneath, and somersaulted down the large mound of landfill landing on my back, I sprang back up running in the direction of the local woods daring to look behind to see if he had given chase. There was no sign of him as I ran towards the entrance of the woods, putting as much distance as possible between us; I sat down exhausted from my sudden burst of energy. My health declining from lack of food and exercise, I tried to gather myself.

That was close to bloody close, I was angry the Bastard tricked me. I was shocked he had been there but what I could not have known or even thought about, he no longer had us to do his dirty work and had to get off his ass and do most things for him self.

my breathing started to slow down a little, the sound of a car engine made me look up I recognized the white van approaching, he was not giving up. I started to run again my chest burning, oh how I wished I did not smoke he chased me into the woods, hot on my heels I squeezed into a small hollow.

He was now in my territory I had spent many nights foraging in the woods when mother was in Canada, I heard him approaching, my heart thumping I was sure he would hear my breathing, I tried to take deep shallow gulps of air he was moving the bushes and hitting them with a large clump of wood.

Shit, he knows I am here closing my eyes the terror to despicable for me to contemplate, I believed I will drop dead from fright opening my eyes as his footsteps echoed into my very being. Step-father came into view and I calmed myself with the knowledge I was able to monitor his movements. Please god keep me concealed, the realization this may be my last place on earth I did not want to die in the dirt, panic coursed through me as my legs buckled and I struggled not to rustle the undergrowth that held my life in its foliage.

I could hear the rushing of a nearby stream, and wished I was in her waters with the debris that she collects. He looked right at me and was close enough for me to touch his face, or so it seemed.

"Look you blind bastard not so clever now are you,"

I cockily thought as I became bolder.

"You are finished bitch I am going to kill you?"

This jolted me back to reality and my smugness of deceiving him waned back to fear, his acid tongue continued I had reached my usefulness and was no longer needed; he was ranting and raving like some one crazed.

He scanned around looking for some clue to where I was hidden.

"You and your asshole brothers, who the fuck did think you were"

Flopping on a tree trunk that had fallen with the resent gales, he knew I was here somewhere.

"You might as well come out and face the music, you are mine bitch but I will wait I love these games"

Trembling, I knew that my life was in my own hands no matter how much he pleaded or threatened I must stay where I was.

"Dick heads, all three of you pissed me right off,"

Still scanning the array of trees waiting for me to make a mistake, a bird flew from a nearby bush it startled him.

I heard footsteps approaching and was going to shout for help but nothing came out, I heard him speak,

"Have you seen a black and white dog?"

I strained to see whom he was speaking to, but my view obstructed by the fullness of my hideaway.

"Ok thanks mate bloody animals, I will keep looking"

Hopelessness once again encased me listening as the footsteps became quieter and ceased to exist.

"Bloody hell why could no one else hear what he is saying" once again he sat down on the trunk ranting and raving

"You see Sharon you are a liar, so fucked in the head that you will lie about your dear old dad."

He let out a blood-curdling laugh I believed he had gone completely insane I had never seen him like this, and wished some one was listening to the conversation.

"COME OUT BITCH" he hissed, I heard more footsteps but was too terrified to call for help. He stood up again

"I am going to stay here until you come out I will be waiting ready to pounce" he continued his vile intentions on my body once caught, I tried to distract away from his degrading renditions towards my corps once he had his way with me he walked out of view.

I waited for what seemed an eternity debating with myself whether to leave the safety of my hide out. Deciding to wait a little longer, a few minutes later I heard the sound of an engine starting up in the distance. Plucking up the courage to leave the safety of my hiding place, I very gradually and cautiously made my way to the place I thought his van would be parked. Fearfully checking all the bushes for signs of him, I started to make my way to the main road changing my mind once again, returning to the security of the woods.

Deciding to leave from another exit that cars had no access to, scrutinizing my surroundings I picked up the biggest stick I could carry, and beat the bushes down to make a pathway knowing that if I had to force my way through the undergrowth, there was no likelihood of him laying in wait, this was exhausting and painful as the brambles ripped at my skin, my hair left on the brambles in clumps lightly floating in the warm summers breeze, giving no hint of my terror as I forced my way through, it was a small price to pay for feeling safe.

I knew it was only a matter of time before he caught me; I had no choice but to leave Devon sooner rather than later.

I also had no perception how to achieve this, no money or job prospects no will to do anything. Making my way to the local beach that would normally take an hour, had taken me three, I was uneasy on the main roads using the back streets I felt like a gutter rat as I dashed from back ally to back ally, for fear of being seen.

The sun was shining I was sixteen years old with the rest of my life before me, I wanted to die and if the truth was known cowardice is all that stopped me. As I entered the fresh smelling atmosphere of the beach I started to feel better, sitting on the grass verge away from the crowds.

Looking out towards the horizon the sun shimmered on the water like glass, I looked around at the people wondering if they were happy, wishing I were part of someone's family. I heard the excited squeals of a little girl and watched as her father playfully chased her. I lay down to soak the suns rays lifting my arms, cleaning them with my own spit, some of the scratches were deep and I watched as the blood spilled from me, if only it were this simple to cleanse my inner soul.

Never had I felt alone as I did this second, loneliness consumed me as my heart became heavier with my sadness, I could feel the emotions inside bubbling to the surface and once again suppressed them, I knew if I started to cry I would probably never stop

Thinking back to where it all begun, time was moving on and dusk was settling, time to go. Time and tiredness had over taken me I must have fell asleep and was annoyed with myself for allowing to succumb to my exhaustion, leaving me vulnerable, I wont ever allow myself to do that again. I stopped to take in the view knowing this was the last time I would see the sun set on this beach.

Walking away I felt a little strange there was a long road for me to travel my life was just beginning. I decided to leave Devon within the next few days. I felt immeasurable sadness at loosing my brothers, once we were three, now there's only me.

Once again I look towards the sea and for a split second doubted my self. It was as though god him self was telling me to go, once again the moonlight lit my way, only this time it was the path of my future. I was unsure were I was going and were I would lay my head in the next few weeks, but I knew I had not gone through the last few months just to be killed by my abuser and buried beneath the soil to rot away with no one to miss me, or mourn my passing.

ABOUT THE AUTHOR

Quoted by S Wallace
My life has always been a bed of roses;
only some one nicked the petals and left me the thorns!

A HOUSE FULL OF WHISPERS WAS WRITTEN BY 49 YEARS old Sharon Wallace, who lives in Devon and is the survivor of the abuse she suffered throughout her young life. She is married and has five grown up sons and along with her grandchildren are the most important things in her life. She has fostered many children along the way and looked after many others when society seemed to forget them, an avid supporter of childrens rights, and a woman who is not afraid to speak out for the ones who have no voice.

She has been writing for thirty years and has poetry published in her local paper and many on line. Sharon is also a keen photographer and has some wonderful frames of scenery from the many places she has travelled. www.sharonwallace.co.uk is the link you can use to samples her works

Surviving a house full of whispers is the second in a trilogy that will be ready in 2007 she believes it is more harrowing than the first because it tells her struggle to gain a place in society and be accepted. The third and final book

Time to let go. Deals with her fight against illness and recognition from her biological father, her life has been anything but un-eventful and reading her story makes one wonder how this woman has survived and become the caring person she is today. An insight into her life will make you experience many emotions; one thought jumps into my mind after reading her book,

Shit happens I am glad I walk in my own shoes and not hers.

Printed in the United Kingdom
by Lightning Source UK Ltd.
115345UKS00001B/316